CIVIL WAR
WINCHESTER

To Stm,

Feb 29, 2012

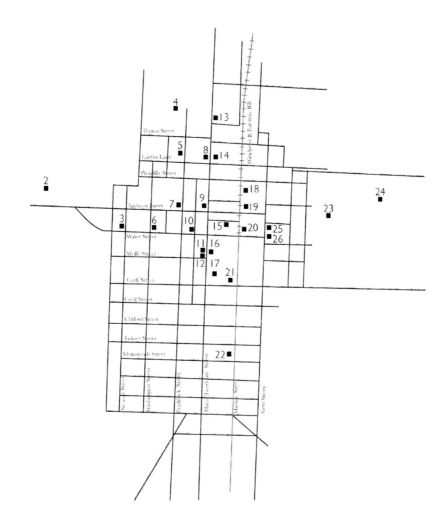

Wartime Winchester. 1) Hawthorne (home of Cornelia McDonald); 2) Selma (home of James Mason); 3) Winchester Medical College; 4) Jackson's headquarters (Lewis T. Moore Home); 5) Kent Street Manse; 6) Christ Episcopal Church; 7) Hunter McGuire Home; 8) Julia Chase Home; 9) Taylor Hotel; 10) Grace Lutheran Church; 11) Tillie Russell Home; 12) Kate Sperry Home; 13) Mary Tucker Magill Home; 14) Rebecca Wright Home; 15) the courthouse; 16) Gettie Miller Home; 17) Loudoun Street Presbyterian Church; 18) Mrs. Mary Lee Home; 19) David Barton Home; 20) Robert Y. Conrad Home; 21) Market Street Methodist Church; 22) John Henry Funk Home; 23) Mount Hebron Cemetery; 24) Stonewall Cemetery; 25) Emma Riley Home; and 26) Kent Street Presbyterian Church. Map based on image drawn by Mary Mayhew.

CIVIL WAR
WINCHESTER

JERRY W. HOLSWORTH

Foreword by Ben Ritter

Charleston   London

THE
History
PRESS

Published by The History Press
Charleston, SC 29403
www.historypress.net

Cover: Confederate Memorial Day, Stonewall Cemetery, Winchester, Virginia. *Courtesy of Kimberly Mauck, Turner Ashby Chapter, UDC.*

First published 2011
Second printing 2011

Manufactured in the United States

ISBN 978.1.60949.161.1

Library of Congress Cataloging-in-Publication Data

Holsworth, Jerry W.
Civil War Winchester / Jerry W. Holsworth.
p. cm.
Includes bibliographical references and index.
ISBN 978-1-60949-161-1
1. Winchester (Va.)--History, Military--19th century. 2. Shenandoah River Valley (Va. and W. Va.)--History--Civil War, 1861-1865. 3. Winchester (Va.)--Social conditions--19th century. I. Title.
F234.W8H65 2011
975.5'99103--dc22
2011011143

Notice: The information in this book is true and complete to the best of our knowledge. It is offered without guarantee on the part of the author or The History Press. The author and The History Press disclaim all liability in connection with the use of this book.

This book is dedicated to Captain Hugh H. McGuire (brother of Dr. Hunter McGuire), Company E, Eleventh Virginia Cavalry, CSA. He died of wounds on May 5, 1865, the last Winchester native to die as a result of combat during the Civil War. He was twenty-three years old.

Contents

Foreword

The story of Winchester, Virginia, in the Civil War is a combination of the best and worst of the war. But the story of the town's role in those important days has paled in comparison to other events of the war. Only three or four books have been written on the subject, and only one is still available for purchase. For those of us who grew up here, it also has the added attraction of being a story in which our families actually participated. Almost every American family can find an ancestor who fought in the war and participated in one or more of the important battles. Few, however, can trace their lineage to this unique story.

Winchester and Frederick County, like most of the Shenandoah Valley, had very little interest in secession or slavery. Our way of life was rooted in a Protestant ethic that had little to do with the antebellum Old South. Founded by Presbyterians, Lutherans, Quakers and Methodists, we were—and to a large extent still are—yeoman farmers. There are no Scarlett O'Haras or Rhett Butlers in this Valley. The war brought suffering and deprivation, but it also revealed the serene courage and strong character that has always been the way of this Valley.

Jerry Holsworth was not born in Winchester, Virginia. He hails from Dallas, Texas, and moved here in 1986 after working as a teacher in the Dallas Independent School District for a dozen years. Like they say, "There's nothing like a convert," and for the past twenty-five years, Jerry has immersed himself in the history of his adopted hometown and has become well versed in not just the Civil War history of Winchester but all of its history.

His work in Winchester has included a three-year stint as manager of the George Washington Office Museum and as a docent at Stonewall Jackson's Headquarters. He also spent a couple of years as a seasonal park ranger at Antietam National Battlefield watching over Miller's Cornfield, where the subject of his other favorite topic, Hood's Texas Brigade, fought.

In between those jobs, he's managed to write several excellent articles on Winchester during the Civil War for *Blue and Gray Magazine* and *Civil War Times*. If that were not enough, he has become one of the most popular tour guides in the Shenandoah Valley, taking buses from all over the country on tours of historic sites from Winchester to Harrisonburg. But his first love is, and always has been, Winchester, and he can be seen several times a year taking tour groups through the streets of Winchester on guided tours of historic sites.

His writing skill, which he developed covering sporting events for our local newspapers, emphasizes good storytelling. For Civil War enthusiasts who love their history and also love to see it presented in an entertaining way, this is the book to buy, and it was a pleasure to work with him on it over the past few months. It is the culmination of almost a quarter-century of digging deep into the history of Winchester for the best stories, which he tells with a flair that few can equal.

Ben Ritter
Winchester, Virginia

Acknowledgements

The story of Winchester in the Civil War could not be presented without recognizing the work of several people, particularly those who have already written about the subject. Margaretta Barton Colt's book *Defend the Valley: A Shenandoah Valley Family at War* chronicles the destruction and eventual resurrection of the Barton and Jones families. A descendant of her subject, she writes straight from the heart, and it is one of the most moving books in Civil War literature. Garland Quarles, former superintendent of the Winchester Public Schools, used his considerable talents as a historian to write several books on the history of his hometown of Winchester, Virginia. Fortunately, his books are still in print thanks to the Winchester–Frederick County Historical Society. The most recent book on the subject, *Beleaguered Winchester: A Virginia Community at War, 1861–1865*, by Richard R. Duncan, is also the most thorough. His research notes, which he kindly donated to the Handley Library, were a very useful source of information.

Ben Ritter, although he rarely writes on the subject, remains Winchester's and Fredrick County's most preeminent historian. For more than sixty years, Ritter has studied the Civil War and its aftermath from the perspective of his hometown. He has also dedicated long hours and countless days to the preservation of that heritage. No historian who wishes to recount the history of Winchester during the Civil War can do so successfully without consulting him. His help on this book was invaluable, and I am deeply grateful for it. Not only did he provide me with a bottomless pit of research material, but he also provided most of the pictures and illustrations for the book from his collection, most of which he inherited from Quarles. They are credited in the text with the abbreviation "GQ/BR."

Wilbur Johnston, who has produced the best maps of Winchester, was kind enough to allow a couple of his creations to be used in this book. With no useable map of downtown Winchester readily available, Mary Mayhew agreed to draw one, and I would like to thank her for the wonderful job she did. None of the maps or pictures would have been possible without the work of Tina Helms, who made sure that each had the right resolution for the book and copied them to a flash drive so that they could be quickly processed by The History Press.

For the rest of the illustrations, I would like to thank Becky Ebert and Cissy Shull. Ebert is the archivist at the Stewart Bell Jr. Archives, Handley Regional Library, in Winchester. The Stewart Bell Jr. Archives contains the largest collection anywhere on Winchester during the Civil War, as well as thousands of pictures of local residents from as far back as the 1700s. Shull, the executive director of the Winchester–Frederick County Historical Society, and Ebert made these limitless sources available to me from the very beginning, and this book would not have been possible without them. Illustrations and pictures used in this book that are from the Stewart Bell Jr. Archives, Handley Regional Library are credited with "THL," and those from the Winchester–Frederick County Historical Society are credited with the abbreviation "WFCHS."

Finally, and perhaps most importantly, I would like to thank my proofreader, Helene Becker. There is not a word of this book that she has not read to make sure that my many typographical errors were removed.

Introduction

Each year on June 6 many people around the world commemorate D-Day, with the television and newspapers filled with reminiscences of the great events that took place on the coast of France that momentous day in 1944. But for a few hundred people in Winchester, Virginia, the focus will not be on the liberation of Europe or anything else that took place in the twentieth century. Every year during the early afternoon of June 6, a large procession of cars journeys from all parts of Frederick County, Virginia, toward the old section of Mount Hebron Cemetery. They come from all walks of life and all political persuasions. They are old and young, male and female, wealthy and humble and Democrat and Republican.

As they meander through the narrow roads, passing the graves of noted celebrities buried in the town's cemetery, they hardly notice luminaries like Daniel Morgan or Harry Flood Byrd. Instead they cast brief glances at the aging tombstones of people almost no one has ever heard of. Names like Mary Greenhow Lee, Stover and Billy Funk, Robert Y. Conrad, James Graham, Frank Jones and Tillie Russell are on their minds today. Heading east, they exit their cars near Stonewall Cemetery, where several thousand small tombstones lie in perfect rows, each marked by a tiny Confederate flag. The crowd walks quietly past them toward a large mound of earth behind the flags.

Underneath that mound are buried the earthly remains of 829 unknown Confederate soldiers who gave their lives in the final battles fought in the Shenandoah Valley during the Civil War. There are the usual handshakes and broad smiles that always accompany a gathering of old friends, but the atmosphere is decidedly sober. Those who wish to do so sit in the metal folding chairs provided for the occasion, but most stand. Bands play period music, prayers are offered and a keynote speaker says a few remarks during the brief but moving ceremony. It is Confederate Memorial Day in Winchester, Virginia.

Most outsiders would see this gathering, particularly in the early twenty-first century, as about as politically incorrect as it could possibly get, but the people here really don't care. They are not here to celebrate states' rights or the defense of slavery or shed tears for the "Lost Cause." They are here for the simplest of all reasons: family. They are here to pay tribute to their own blood kin who suffered through four years of living hell during the Civil War and who bore it with dignity and grace, as well as to say thank you to several thousand young men who 150 years ago, from as close as across the street to as far away as Texas and Florida, gave their lives to protect the little town of Winchester.

Ask the people who live in Winchester today who were the greatest heroes of the Civil War, and you will rarely hear names like Robert E. Lee, Jefferson Davis or "Jeb" Stuart. Ask them who the enemy was, and you will hardly ever hear names such as Abraham Lincoln, Ulysses S. Grant or William T. Sherman, despite the citizens' strong Southern leanings. The names that will invariably come up are almost completely unknown outside the city limits of Winchester. Heyward Shepherd, Robert Y. and Holmes Conrad, Mary Greenhow Lee, Kate Sperry, Philip Williams, Andrew Boyd and Cornelia McDonald are the heroes they will mention. They have their share of villains, too. Names like Nathaniel Banks, Robert Milroy, David Hunter and Philip Sheridan usually head their list of scoundrels.

A closer look explains much about their attitude. Winchester, despite its decidedly Union sentiments before secession, became the most fought-over town of the war. Most historians believe that the town changed hands at least seventy-two times, and many believe that the number is closer to ninety. There were seven major engagements within Frederick County, including the two bloodiest battles fought in the Shenandoah Valley. Occupying armies, even friendly ones, consumed enormous resources and left the area an unsanitary nightmare.

Winchester and Frederick County, despite their lack of enthusiasm for the issues that caused the war, were forced by simple geography to play an important role in it. The Shenandoah Valley was of such strategic importance on several different levels that it was inevitable that it would become a major battleground. Situated on a series of road networks that included the famed Valley Pike and a rickety, but vital, railroad, Winchester was the key to holding the Valley.

From the Confederate standpoint, Winchester was just twenty miles south of the Baltimore and Ohio Railroad and just a few miles more from the Chesapeake and Ohio Canal, both of which were indispensable connections between midwestern wheat and coal and the eastern seaboard. Southern forces used Winchester, whenever they could hold it, for raids on those supply links, with devastating effect.

The Shenandoah Valley was also an avenue of invasion that was used twice on a large scale to threaten both Washington, D.C., and the important railroad that traveled through Harrisburg, Pennsylvania. Winchester was actually geographically north of Washington, D.C., and Confederate armies and raiding parties could hide behind the Blue Ridge Mountains and be in Pennsylvania or Maryland quickly. In both 1863 and 1864, Confederate armies used Winchester as the launching point for an invasion of the North, as well as a sanctuary in retreat when those excursions failed.

From the Union viewpoint, Winchester was equally important for both offensive and defensive reasons. A sufficiently large Union force in Winchester effectively blocked any offensive thrust north from the Shenandoah Valley and could keep a close eye on guerrilla activities in the area that might threaten Union railroad and canal links.

The Shenandoah Valley was the "Breadbasket of the Confederacy," keeping General Robert E. Lee's Army of Northern Virginia with food and fodder throughout the war. Winchester was the perfect jumping-off point for capturing or destroying these supplies and threatening the Virginia Central Railroad at Staunton, just eighty miles south, which carried those supplies to Lee's army.

The biggest problem for both armies was actually defending the crucial crossroads town. Surrounded by hills, attacking armies held all of the advantages in any battle fought at or near Winchester. Avenues of approach were also almost inexhaustible, and several were used with great success throughout the war. Both sides built forts and fortifications in an attempt to aid in defense, but few, if any, proved to be effective. With one exception and despite innumerable attempts by both sides, no one was able to successfully defend Winchester from attack when a determined effort was made to take the town.

For a town of only 4,400 inhabitants, many of whom were away in the army, the almost continuous grappling of these contending armies was close to an impossible situation. The combined forces that fought major battles and countless skirmishes here were sometimes ten to fifteen times the population of the town, and dealing with the aftermath of those battles was an overwhelming task. Teenage girls—who just months before had been enjoying the town's social life and the normal courting process that they hoped would someday turn them into wives and mothers—were now kneeling helplessly by fresh mounds of dirt where their future husbands' mortal remains were buried.

These same girls, along with their mothers and grandmothers, were, without any training, forced to transform themselves into nurses for the thousands of wounded soldiers from both sides who remained after the bloodlettings. Homes were turned into hospitals, and backyards were used as cemeteries for the dead from both armies. It is little wonder that just two years after the war was over both the Stonewall Cemetery and the National Cemetery were dedicated. Except for Gettysburg National Cemetery, they were the first cemeteries of their kind dedicated after the war.

The residents of Winchester and Frederick County today, when asked about the community's heroes during the war, will invariably reply with a list of women. The story of these indomitable women of Winchester is the story of the war in the Lower Shenandoah Valley. Whether they were Union or Confederate, they were singularly determined to do their duty, and their actions often went beyond the accepted role of women during that era. These acts invariably brought retaliation, which they bore stoically only when forced to do so.

Unfortunately, what these women endured during the Civil War is a subject rarely recorded by the noted historians of the war. Most of the accounts are of the great battles, leaders and storied campaigns. There are untold volumes on the three-day battle at Gettysburg but almost nothing about the months and years of anguish experienced by that town in the aftermath of those three days. That story is not about charges and countercharges but rather about suffering, heartbreak and perseverance among civilians whose names are lost to history.

The story of Winchester's suffering during the Civil War is an exception. It is fully documented by the very people who endured it. More than a dozen women, ranging in age from their late forties to as young as thirteen, kept diaries of the events they witnessed. There are also hundreds of letters that have survived plus newspaper articles published in the local papers after the war, all of which give great detail into the suffering behind the events of the war. Some chroniclers were dedicated Unionists and others die-hard Rebels, giving the story balance.

The citizens of the Lower Shenandoah Valley who faced this onslaught of both Union and Confederate armies during the war were very different from their counterparts on the east side of the Blue Ridge Mountains. Most were not from English stock, which made up most of the citizenry east of the mountains. These Virginians had migrated south through Pennsylvania and were primarily German and Scotch-Irish, as well as Presbyterian and Lutheran rather than Episcopalian. Those English families who settled in the Valley, unlike the Tidewater and Piedmont regions, were "dissenters" and attended Quaker and Methodist churches.

The pioneers who settled the Shenandoah Valley in the mid-eighteenth century were at best indifferent to their Anglican neighbors and were openly hostile in some cases. They traveled to the New World not as Englishmen but rather for the land and religious freedom. Although their farms were much smaller than the large plantations east of the Blue Ridge, their success as farmers is measured by the Valley's lasting nickname as "Breadbasket of the Confederacy."

They also, for the most part, abhorred slavery, choosing instead to work their farms with their own labor. The Quakers in the area were almost certainly involved in the Underground Railroad movement. When the secession crisis came in 1860, these small farmers and shopkeepers threw their lot almost completely on the side of the Union. Only when the prospect of invasion became a reality did the majority embrace secession. Their leaders fought hard to keep the Old Dominion in the Union, even after Virginia's Secession Convention voted otherwise. But when war came, they were also prepared to defend what they had fought for more than a century to build.

For their descendants, who travel home to their jobs and families after the ceremony on June 6, it is a story that is deeply personal—Winchester's journey through the crucible of war is also their story. The four years of suffering proved too much for many of the town's residents—these chose to leave rather than face the arduous task ahead of them. Most, however, stayed, endured and eventually rebuilt their shattered town. In the end, the Confederacy proved a failure, but Winchester did not. The successful lives of those who participate in the memorial service at Stonewall Cemetery each year are a lasting testament to a few hundred women, old men and children who persevered and triumphed in the face of the intensely personal tragedy that was Winchester during the Civil War.

Chapter 1

"Virginia Right or Wrong"

It was a quiet evening, like most evenings in the Lower Shenandoah Valley. The vast majority of small farmers and merchants in the town of Harpers Ferry had long since gone to bed, while Heyward Shepherd, an employee of the Winchester and Potomac Railroad, made his rounds as a night watchman just after midnight on October 17, 1859. The short line of track that joined with the Baltimore and Ohio Railroad at Harpers Ferry connected the Lower Shenandoah Valley's rich produce with the rest of the United States. The free African American must have been happy for the work, since he had eight children in addition to a wife to feed in his nearby hometown of Winchester, Virginia.

When Shepherd heard a commotion near the bridge where the Baltimore and Ohio Railroad crossed the Potomac River, he went to investigate. Seeing armed men near the bridge, he sensed danger and ran. A voice cried out, which he ignored, and then a gunshot rang out. Shepherd fell, shot through the back. He died the next morning, never really understanding what had happened. Shepherd's unfortunate demise was certainly an ironic twist in what became the bloodiest period of United States history. The men near the bridge were followers of John Brown, and Shepherd's death marked the beginning of Brown's attempt to free the slaves in the South. The fact that the first act of violence by these abolitionists was to kill a free black man seemed lost on them.

It was not, however, lost on the South. The violent and sudden attack by Brown had the same effect on the South that September 11, 2001, had a century and a half later. Passionate disagreement over the issue of slavery was nothing new in the United States, but a carefully planned attack that seemed to have the warm approval of many Northerners was shocking. Among Brown's papers was a call for the extermination of white Southerners and the creation of a "Negro" Republic.

For the citizens of Shepherd's hometown, the event was chilling. The Shenandoah Valley had never been a hotbed of slavery. Settled in the 1730s by Germans, Scotch-Irish and Quakers from Pennsylvania, they did not share the mentality of the landed gentry east of the Blue Ridge. Similar in size and culture to the other counties and towns in the Shenandoah Valley, they were yeoman farmers and proud of it. Frederick County, Virginia, only had 2,300 slaves out of a population of about 16,000, and 655 of the 4,400 residents of the county seat, Winchester, were free blacks. For Shepherd, an African American, to be murdered in cold blood was considered a terrifying statement about the utter ruthlessness of the abolitionist movement. He was buried in the local colored cemetery with much fanfare, and the town council voted to create a special relief fund for the bereaved widow and her family.

John Brown. *GQ/BR.*

"Virginia Right or Wrong"

While Winchester reeled in reaction to Brown's raid, some local citizens used the event for their own purposes. Students from the Winchester Medical College journeyed to Harpers Ferry, stuffed several dead raiders in barrels and took them back to the college as cadavers. The first of its kind in Virginia, the medical college was founded by Dr. Hugh Holmes McGuire. His son, Dr. Hunter McGuire, was an instructor there and later became "Stonewall" Jackson's personal physician. Although only a few of these cadavers were ever positively identified, many believed that one of them was a son of John Brown's. The college paid a terrible price for these students' ingenuity when the Union army occupied the town in March 1862.

For the rest of Winchester, Brown's raid and the support it received from many Northerners was terrifying. Slave revolts, although uncommon, did happen, and the last major one in Virginia, featuring Nat Turner, had been particularly bloody. Whether one was for or against slavery, an abolitionist plot that included the genocide of all white Southerners could not be ignored. It was also hard not to believe that the citizens of the Shenandoah Valley had been targeted by Brown and his raiders. Three local militia companies

Judge Richard Parker, a Frederick County, Virginia judge who presided over the John Brown trial. *GQ/BR.*

from Winchester and Frederick County left for Harpers Ferry within twenty-four hours of Brown's appearance and participated in his capture. When the conspirators were tried in November, Frederick County judge Richard Parker was selected to oversee Brown's trial. After many Northern newspapers called for a vigilante effort to help Brown escape, Winchester's militia companies were again called up for duty to guard the prisoner until his execution in early December.

Just a year later, two more events increased tensions. Abraham Lincoln, a sectional candidate who opposed the expansion of slavery, was nominated for president by the Republican Party. The Democratic Party split into three factions during its 1860 convention. Despite several attempts, no sectional candidate for president had been successful, but with the breakup of the Democratic Party the likelihood of a sectional candidate being elected was significantly increased. This left everyone in the South wondering what the election of Lincoln might mean. Secession would almost certainly become a reality, at least in the Deep South, if Lincoln was elected.

For Winchester, the issue was clear to most people. The railroad and the network of roads linked their economy with the North, and they were Unionist in their sentiments. But they also strongly believed that the South had good reason for concern over a candidate like Lincoln. On the heels of Brown's raid, fear of slave revolt was heightened by the election of Lincoln, and the majority fell into the category of "Conditional Unionists." The 1860 election in Frederick County and Winchester clearly demonstrated just how conditional that support was. John C. Breckinridge, the most hard-line of the three Democratic candidates, won an overwhelming victory in Frederick County, while Winchester was a dead heat between John Bell, the Constitutional Union Party candidate, and Breckinridge. Only one vote, by Quaker Joseph Jolliffe, was cast for Lincoln.

When Lincoln won, the argument intensified. The two local newspapers, the *Winchester Republican* and the *Winchester Virginian*, took opposing sides on the issue of secession. Feelings were running high when on December 14, 1860, Unionist Robert Y. Conrad stepped forward to speak at a pubic rally at the courthouse. The respected local lawyer and former state senator warned that the call for secession was "threatening speedy destruction of our Union and Constitution" and that it meant civil war and "the loss to civilized man of all hope of securing peace, liberty, and happiness, by a representative republican form of civil government."

Conrad's words had a calming effect, but only for a brief time. Less than a week later, South Carolina seceded, and other states in the Deep South seemed ready to follow it. This brought on a new series of rallies as citizens grappled with how to react to this. Winchester's James Mason was the grandson of George Mason and was, as a United States senator and author of the 1850 Fugitive Slave Act, fervently for secession. Local Quakers, as well as many artisans and mechanics, were equally opposed to leaving the Union. Two more rallies took place in early January 1861. One declared that "no state, or combination of states, of the Federal Union can absolve herself of her duty to her co-states." Another rally took a decidedly different position, stating, "When the hour of trial does come we will be found standing firmly by the Constitutional rights of the Southern states."

Emotions were overflowing into the streets, and Governor John Letcher, a resident of the Shenandoah Valley and a Unionist, was forced to respond. He called for a special session of the legislature to meet on January 19, 1861, to determine Virginia's position. He also proposed that a conference of states be organized to search for a compromise that would avoid the breakup of the Union. Letcher set February 13, 1861, as the date for the opening of the convention and February 9 for the election of delegates. To complicate matters, before the election was held, six states from the Deep South seceded. The contest in Frederick County was fierce. Frederick Holliday and William Clark ran as secession candidates, while Conrad and James Marshall ran on a Unionist platform.

Marshall—the nephew of former Supreme Court justice John Marshall and the grandson of founding father Robert Morris—added considerable prestige to the ticket, but it was Conrad who was the leader of the Unionist camp. The fifty-six-year-old had left West Point as a young man to pursue law in his hometown and had risen to be one of the most respected citizens in the community. His stance against secession was consistent and attractive to the citizens of Frederick County who wanted to find an honorable way out of the crisis. He was, however, no admirer of Lincoln, whom he blamed for the calamity that the country now faced.

Just before the election, Conrad and Marshall issued a joint statement in the *Winchester Republican* that put the blame on both parties: "The continued existence of this party [Republican] is inconsistent with the safety and permanence of our Union because it is necessarily confined to one portion of the States, and, if in a majority, would establish permanent rule over the other section." Conrad also stated that the secessionists in the South "furnish no cure, but only aggravate the evils of which we complain." With sentiments like these, Conrad and Marshall easily defeated the secessionist candidates on February 9.

Conrad's first act as a delegate to the convention, which began on February 13, was to propose that a committee on federal relations be formed to consider all matters concerning the federal government. The measure was unanimously adopted, and Conrad was made chairman. Since the purpose of the convention was to respond to the actions or possible actions of the Lincoln administration, this moved Conrad to the position of one of the most important leaders of the Unionist movement at the convention. Shortly before the vote for delegates to the Virginia Convention, former Democratic presidential candidate Stephen A. Douglas stated that "[a]ll depends on the actions of Virginia and the Border States. Save Virginia, and we save the Union." As chairman of the all-important Federal Relations Committee, the salvation of the Union and the avoidance of civil war now rested, in large measure, on the shoulders of Robert Y. Conrad of Winchester, Virginia.

Robert Y. Conrad, Winchester–Frederick County's representative to the Virginia Secession Convention who led the fight to keep Virginia in the Union. *GQ/BR.*

"Virginia Right or Wrong"

One thing working in Conrad's favor was the makeup of the convention. The secessionists represented only about one-third of the delegates and would be forced to maneuver carefully to take Virginia out of the Union. The remaining delegates were either committed Unionists or, like Conrad, "Conditional Unionists." In the Federal Relations Committee, there were only three secessionists to four unionists and ten moderates. Their initial advantage might have been short-lived though. Virginia considered itself a Southern state and would never take an action that might be interpreted as siding against its sister states in the South, and there was always the possibility that events elsewhere might force Virginia's hand.

The secessionists knew this, and they employed delaying tactics, hoping that some action of Lincoln, the seceded states or both would force the issue. Unfortunately for Conrad and his Unionist allies, events did begin to unfold almost immediately that reduced their chances of averting secession and war. Conrad's correspondence with his wife revealed his frustrations, his fatigue at the mountain of work that needed to be performed and his determination to get the job done. On February 18, he confided: "The Committee on Federal Relations has the whole work of the convention to do, and as their chairman, that work has devolved upon me. I yet trust we shall succeed in our objections, though the storm rages as fiercely as ever."

The secessionist minority, led by former governor Henry A. Wise, blocked and delayed every attempt by Conrad to finish the committee's work. On March 2, he wrote to his wife: "I trust we will be able to report next week—if my friend [Wise]—will allow us. He makes elaborate speeches upon every proposition or suggestion, agrees to nothing, and proposed nothing practicable himself." The secessionist tactics were not limited to delay but also included attempts to intimidate the delegates. On March 6, Conrad wrote, "Outside pressure both from the members of the convention and the popular clamor, is very great. Mobs assemble every night."

Stymied from within and without, the first of a series of events occurred that eventually undermined Conrad's work. Lincoln's inaugural address made clear his resolve to hold and defend all federal installations within the seceded states. Did he mean that the forts now under federal control would remain so, or did he intend to use force to retake the ones already seized? Conrad acknowledged that Lincoln's inaugural "came upon us like an earthquake" and that "Lincoln's position has embarrassed and changed somewhat our movements."

Conrad was still confident in ultimate success, although a lukewarm reception of the Virginia peace commission by the U.S. Congress and

Lincoln did not help matters. Throughout these difficult days, he still received warm support from the *Winchester Republican.* In its March 8 issue, it noted that Lincoln's position on secession was no different from "Madison, Webster, Jackson, Clay, and Buchanan" and blamed the failure of the peace commission on "extremists," including Winchester native and Virginia senator James M. Mason.

When the Foreign Relations Committee finally made its report on March 9, it set off an almost endless debate. Its seventeen provisions stressed states' rights, the right of secession and the legality of slavery. When on April 4 the convention finally arrived at the sixth provision, Amelia County delegate Lewis Edwin Harvie offered a substitute provision for immediate secession. When the vote was taken, Conrad and the Unionists won a stunning victory. Even after the aggravation caused by Lincoln's inaugural, Harvie's provision was voted down eighty-eight to forty-five. Just eight days later, though, an event several hundred miles away completely destroyed Conrad's endless hours of work.

The United States was seventy years old in 1861, whereas all of the thirteen original states had been in existence since the 1600s. Virginia, the oldest, was founded in 1607 and was almost two hundred years older than the U.S. Constitution. Naturally, Virginians held a longer and stronger loyalty to their state than to the Union. The Constitution also seemed to endorse secession. The Tenth Amendment specifically stated that powers not expressly given to the federal government automatically belonged to the states and the people. Nowhere in the Constitution did it give the federal government the power to coerce any state to stay in the Union. The delegates at the 1861 Virginia Convention, including Conrad, strongly believed this. Whether Virginia seceded or not, they would never support any effort by the federal government to force the seceded states back into the Union.

On April 12, the one thing that Conrad feared most happened. When Lincoln attempted to reinforce the federal garrison at Fort Sumter in Charleston Harbor, Confederate forces fired on the fort, forcing its surrender. Just days later, Lincoln called on the states to provide 75,000 troops to put down the rebellion. Virginia's allotment was to be about 2,500 men. Secessionist James M. Mason, from his home in Winchester, stated, "This ends the question; Virginia will at once secede." Mason was right, and on April 17 the convention voted eighty-eight to fifty-five to secede. Conrad and Marshall still voted against the measure, as did most of the delegates from the Shenandoah Valley. Of the seventeen Valley delegates, twelve voted against secession after Fort Sumter and Lincoln's call for troops. Although

James Mason, grandson
of George Mason and
leading secessionist in
Winchester, Virginia.
GQ/BR.

the measure had to be approved by a vote of the people, few believed that the citizens of the Old Dominion would reject it, and on May 23 Virginia voted more than four to one for secession.

But even before the votes of the convention and the general public were in, efforts were already being made to defend the state against invasion. Militia forces were moving through Winchester as early as April 17 on the way to Harpers Ferry to seize the arsenal there. Governor Letcher even wired the president of the Baltimore and Ohio Railroad that if the railroad was used to transport federal troops from the West to Washington or Baltimore, he would order the railroad seized.

In Winchester, the change in attitude was swift and dramatic. Cornelia McDonald was shocked to see that "[w]hen I got to town every person I met was full of joy; those who a week ago were so violently opposed to secession had completely turned around." McDonald, who was one of several women in town who kept diaries throughout the war, was a close friend of both Mason and Conrad. The second wife of Angus McDonald, she was just short of forty years old when Virginia seceded. Her sixty-two-year-old husband, who was a graduate of West Point, organized a cavalry company shortly after Virginia seceded, leaving her alone to care for seven children, all under the age of fourteen.

Soldiers marching through town received enthusiastic support from almost everyone. Wild celebrations, complete with young girls waving Confederate or Virginia flags, greeted every company that passed through. McDonald said that they were from "all points of the state, men of all grades and pursuits, farmers from their ploughs, boys from their schools, students from the colleges, all were making to the point of expected conflict." Among the rallies and speeches and flag-draped buildings, the passing troops reveled in Winchester's "lavish hospitality." The excitement was contagious, and three more militia companies were raised within the county. A group of local boys known as the "Boomerangs" journeyed to Harpers Ferry and enlisted in several companies that eventually became the Thirteenth Virginia Infantry. Local companies with names like the Mountain Rangers and the Newtown Light Dragoons all marched to Harpers Ferry to repel the invaders.

The women in town formed knitting societies to sew socks, caps, clothing and bandages for the new recruits. Local merchants provided them with the raw materials, and the town council passed a bill providing for the relief of

Confederate troops assembling at the Market House on Market Street in 1861. *GQ/BR.*

families whose loved ones were away in the army. Soldiers from as far away as Mississippi and Alabama were treated with the same enthusiasm as boys from Virginia, and the girls in town vied with one another to pay tribute to the new volunteers. With the sudden influx of soldiers, housing became an acute problem, as there were not nearly enough tents for the thousands who passed through town. Emma Riely, a fourteen-year-old girl who lived on Kent Street just two blocks from downtown, wrote that "the patriotic citizens could not see them turned out on Mother Earth with nothing but the sky to cover them, so they sent word to the quartermaster to divide them out among the people." She continued: "Many a night, every bed, as well as the floors of the house, were filled with soldiers."

Kate McVicar, a teenage girl living just north of town, stated years later that "[n]o one thought of the possible dangers that might come to their families by allowing them to have free intercourse with these strangers." She added: "Many youthful romances began then that were ended by the heart of the soldier being stilled in death." The formerly Unionist *Winchester Republican* even got into the act, commenting that "the entire population, old and young—men, women, and children, negroes and all—are in arms, ready to march at a moment's warning." The few Unionists left in town kept to themselves and avoided doing anything that might attract attention. Fearing reprisals, many stayed at home when the election on secession took place. Conrad, who remained in Richmond several months after the vote, was seen by many as lacking patriotism. When he and Marshall ran for the state legislature in early May, they were both decisively defeated.

Two days after the convention voted for secession, Conrad wrote his wife, "You may imagine how heavily it has pressed upon me:—never before have I felt such a weight upon my brain and my heart. No dawn of hope appears to show us how to avert the calamity of civil war." He continued, saying that "[t]he danger, however, is so imminent, and the minds of all on both sides just now so much excited, that, at present, we have only to consider the means of defense." While many in his hometown questioned his judgment, not to mention his loyalty, Conrad worked closely with Letcher, newly appointed commander of Virginia forces, General Robert E. Lee and Colonel Thomas J. Jackson, who was shortly to be put in command of the recruits assembling at Harpers Ferry, to see that everything was done to protect the Valley.

Reluctantly, Conrad now took his place as the leader of a community at war. His sons had either enlisted or were in the process of enlisting into Confederate service. When the official document of secession was finally presented to the convention, Conrad signed it. As a representative of his people, it was now his duty to join them and endure with them the uncertain future that lay ahead. Despite his strong aversion to secession, he completely agreed with the slogan written on the flag of one of the local militia companies. On the banner of the Marion Rifles (commanded by newly elected captain John H.S. Funk), soon to become Company A, Fifth Virginia Infantry, was the motto "Virginia, right or wrong: she is our mother, and accursed of God and man is the hand that does not defend her."

Chapter 2

"There Stands Jackson Like a Stone Wall"

I n the midst of the war hysteria that engulfed Winchester, there was also a growing tragedy that became more intense as the war progressed. A minority consistently supported the Union throughout the war. The Civil War has been called a war of "Brother against Brother," and this was nowhere more true than in Winchester. Families, neighbors, business associates and fellow church members were divided over the issue of secession. Many lifelong friendships became casualties. Robert Y. Conrad, who now supported secession, refused to cordially interact with former friends who still remained loyal to the Union. Four of his five sons were either in the Confederate military or would be shortly. When Unionist Boyd Pendleton offered to shake hands early in the war, Conrad "put his hands in his pocket and walked on."

The two most eloquent Unionist voices in Winchester were diarists Julia Chase and Harriet Griffith. Neither did anything that could be remotely defined as treason, but their stance for the Union was clear and adamant. Their two diaries are fair and as accurate as could be expected under the circumstances. Both suffered alongside their Confederate neighbors all of the heartache that war brought to their town.

Chase was born in Maine in 1831 but at the time of the Civil War resided on North Loudoun Street with her parents. Her father, Charles S. Chase, was the postmaster for Winchester and an ardent Unionist. Living on the main thoroughfare gave her an excellent view of troop movements, and historians lean heavily on her diary to determine how many times Winchester changed

Harriet Griffith, a Quaker girl and Unionist who kept a diary during the war. *THL.*

Andrew Boyd, pastor of Loudoun Street Presbyterian Church. *GQ/BR.*

hands. The family were active members of the Loudoun Street Presbyterian Church and fast friends with its pastor, devoted secessionist Andrew H. Boyd. Her father and Boyd debated issues facing the town and the country at her home frequently but cordially. Their differing beliefs concerning the war, however, proved to be fatal to both of them.

Despite their strong Unionist sentiments, the Chase family fed and occasionally entertained Confederate soldiers who were stationed in town. Her father feared that the war would be a long one and thought that he would not live to see its end. Julia confided in her diary that "[t]his will be the worst of wars probably that has ever taken place in the world" and lamented the "sad condition our beloved country has fallen."

Griffith, the teenage daughter of Aaron Griffith and Mary Hollingsworth, was a descendant of Winchester's original settler, Abraham Hollingsworth. Both families were Quakers, antislavery and devoted Unionists. Harriet's father owned the Brookland Woolen Mill just east of town, which he had purchased from Robert Y. Conrad in 1839. The mill was one of the few, if not the only one, to continue operations during the war.

Harriett had sentiments similar to Chase's. In her first diary entry, she wrote, "Our loved and honored America, this our beautiful country, is now at arms. Brother warring against brother, and what for." While the townspeople who supported secession were rejoicing in the streets, Griffith continued, "My heart is sad, very sad, this morning." Later she stated, "Oh, what a state of things, what a trial we have to bear, and this is only the beginning." Events were unfolding just a few miles north at Harpers Ferry that justified their worst fears.

While Chase and Griffith were lamenting the state of the country, their Confederate neighbors were cheering on the new recruits heading toward Harpers Ferry. Neither understood that their town was about to become a battleground, nor the suffering that it would entail. However, one person did. After taking command at Harpers Ferry, Colonel Thomas J. Jackson wrote Congressman Alexander Boteler that "[i]f the Valley is lost, Virginia is lost." A professor at the Virginia Military Institute at Lexington, Virginia, Jackson was to become a legendary figure in the Valley. In April 1861, however, he was almost unknown except to a few former cadets from the institute who were at Harpers Ferry. If the new recruits relied on the opinion of most of his former students, he was probably seen as a source of humor rather than as a competent leader. One former cadet from Winchester, Marshall Barton, referred to Jackson as "a hell of a fool" in a letter he wrote to his cousin in 1855. In fact, Jackson's nickname among the cadets at VMI was "Tom Fool."

Shenandoah Valley, drawn by Wilbur Johnston. *WFCHS.*

Jackson's father-in-law from his first marriage, Dr. George Junkin, had a very different and much more accurate opinion. An ardent Unionist, Junkin resigned as president of Washington College in Lexington shortly after secession and moved to Pennsylvania. On his way north, the respected Presbyterian minister stopped to rest his horses at the Winchester home of Lloyd Logan. While there, he called Jackson "the best and bravest man I have ever known." Junkin added, "[I]f there is a war, as I fear, I tell you, Major Jackson, if his life is spared, will be among its most distinguished heroes."

Jackson, however, remained in command at Harpers Ferry for less than a month. Confederate authorities in Richmond replaced him with General Joseph E. Johnston. A West Point classmate of Robert E. Lee's, Johnston almost immediately became concerned about his ability to defend Harpers Ferry and asked his superiors for permission to withdraw to Winchester. He had several good reasons for that opinion. Harpers Ferry was surrounded by dominating heights, which made it impossible to defend, and two Federal armies were closing on his position. One, under General Robert Patterson, was being assembled north of Harpers Ferry, and another threatened Romney, Virginia, to the west. Either force could easily flank Harpers Ferry or place it under siege by occupying the heights that dominated the town. After receiving permission, Johnston began his retreat on June 13, setting up his headquarters at the Taylor Hotel in downtown Winchester.

Johnston's retreat brought home many of the town's young men who had left just a few weeks before. The joyous effect of the arrival of so many loved ones was immediate. On Market Street, three families welcomed home sons who were in the army. Robert Y. Conrad not only had the pleasure of welcoming home his sons, Holmes, Powell and Daniel, but also his two nephews, Holmes and Tucker A. Conrad, who were the sons of his brother, Dr. Daniel Conrad of Martinsburg. Dr. Conrad, like his brother, was an ardent Unionist before secession. Unlike his brother, Dr. Conrad remained a Unionist after Virginia left the Union. Despite their father's stance, his two sons had secreted off and enlisted.

Conrad's neighbors, David Barton and his wife, Fanny, welcomed home their sons, Marshall, David, Randolph and Strother, as well as their son-in-law, Thomas Marshall, and Fanny's brother, Frank Jones. Marshall and Jones were serving on the staff of Brigadier General Jackson. Only two of the six brothers were not with Johnston's army. Robert Barton had tried to enlist but was discharged for disability, and the youngest, Bolling, was a cadet at VMI. Their neighbor, John N. Bell, welcomed home his son, and namesake, who was one of the Boomerangs and serving with the Thirteenth Virginia Infantry.

Just down the street, Christopher and Eliza Funk were reconnected with their two sons, John Henry and Jefferson, who was called "Billy" by family and friends. John Henry, a recent graduate of the Winchester Medical College and a practicing physician in Marion County when Virginia seceded, had returned to Winchester to enlist and was serving as the company commander of Company A, Fifth Virginia Infantry. Billy was a private in his company.

Private George W. Kurtz, who lived just a few blocks away and was welcomed home by his parents, Isaac and Frances Kurtz, was appropriately a member of the Morgan Continental Guard (now Company K, Fifth Virginia Infantry) since he was the grandson of Adam Kurtz, a member of General Daniel Morgan's famed Virginia Riflemen during the Revolutionary War. Hundreds of others also returned to the joy of their families and friends.

Captain George W. Kurtz in his Morgan Continental Guard uniform. *GQ/BR.*

Although not from Winchester, Dr. Enoch Hunt arrived with the Second Mississippi Infantry as its surgeon. One of the most prolific Winchester diarists was eighteen-year-old Kate Sperry. With her father away working as a sutler, she and her sister lived with her grandfather, Peter Sperry, on Loudoun Street. Since the arrival of the first soldiers to town, the beautiful and vivacious teenager had been entertaining a large number of new suitors and recorded her opinion of them in her diary. She did not hold out much hope for Dr. Hunt when he visited her home. Her only comment was: "[A] real nice fellow—most too good for me."

Despite the town's elation, the arrival of several thousand Confederate soldiers also brought their first real introduction to the consequences of being occupied by an army, even a friendly one. Johnston's army brought a large number of sick soldiers who needed care, as well as several thousand mouths to feed. During the first year of the war, both sides experienced a series of epidemics brought on by soldiers gathering in tightly packed areas to drill and train. Almost immediately, measles, mumps, typhoid fever, scarlet fever, pneumonia and an occasional case of smallpox began to take their tolls.

Second Mississippi Infantry marching past the Taylor Hotel in Winchester, Virginia, in 1861. Dr. Enoch Hunt, Kate Sperry's future husband, was a surgeon in this regiment. *GQ/BR.*

Reverend Benjamin F. Brooke, pastor of Market Street Methodist Church, estimated the number of sick in town at two thousand. Johnston estimated that the average regiment under his command was reduced by sickness to no more than five hundred out of the normal one thousand. Exacerbating the problem was the inexperience of local townspeople in caring for such a large number of sick, the poor state of medicine during the nineteenth century and the unsanitary conditions in the camps.

The soldiers, however, were not the only ones to suffer. In June 1861, Winchester began to experience an unusually high loss of citizens due to disease. It was a problem that got worse as the war progressed. The town that changed hands more times than any other during the war also seemed to change epidemics almost as fast. It was rare when Winchester was not experiencing an outbreak of one disease or another, and almost daily some family suffered a fatality. This was particularly true among the very young and the very old.

On July 4, 1861, Julia Chase recorded that "[t]here are a great many sick in town" and that "numbers have died." Cornelia McDonald, referring to the soldiers from the Deep South, stated that "the hospitals are filling up with sick men from the Southern regiments." She added, "The ladies organized parties for attending to the sick, making clothes for the soldiers, preparing bandages, lint, etc." Market Street Methodist Church was forced to cancel services in order to open the church to 250 sick soldiers.

Even the Quakers, who were the most openly and consistently Unionist, opened their meeting hall to sick Confederates. Harriet Griffith commented on June 16 that when she and her family arrived at the Hopewell Quaker Church for their quarterly meeting, "the house had been pressed last night as a hospital, that 450 soldiers were expected any minute."

At that time, churches in the United States were a uniting force within their communities. There were eleven churches in Winchester at the time of the Civil War, and their leaders played a decisive role in how the town reacted to and survived the war. Caring for the sick and wounded, as well as reinforcing the town's morale and commitment to the cause, whether it was Union or Confederate, required an enormous amount of determination. Their work was a daily challenge that grew as the war progressed.

The courage and determination of these men of the cloth, however, came with an enormous price. Most of the churches were severely damaged by the influx of so many soldiers, and several were totally unusable after the war. Several pastors were not only subjected to indignities by occupying armies but also had their houses searched and their churches used as latrines and stables, and some were even arrested and sent to prison.

Despite the large number of sick soldiers, Winchester had been spared so far from the trauma of battlefield casualties. That changed in late June 1861 with the death of Captain Richard Ashby, company commander of Company A, Seventh Virginia Cavalry. His scouting party was ambushed near the Potomac River, and Ashby was mortally wounded. Richard was well liked by the townspeople, and his death was a shock. It also stirred his brother, Turner, who was lieutenant colonel of the regiment and a renowned horseman, into a furious rage since Richard's body had been mutilated during the fight. He turned that rage into a drive that made him one of the most legendary cavalry figures of the war.

On July 2, newly appointed brigadier general Stonewall Jackson and his brigade fought a skirmish near Falling Waters that resulted in a few minor casualties, who arrived in town along with several hundred Union prisoners. This gave the town a glimpse of what was to come. As the days of summer passed, it became obvious that minor events like these were only the first rumblings of something much worse to come. That something began on July 18 when General Johnston received orders to take his army and move as quickly as possible to Manassas. Confederate forces there, under General

"There Stands Jackson Like a Stone Wall"

P.G.T. Beauregard, were being pressed by a Union army under General Irwin McDowell, and a major battle was imminent. If reinforcements did not arrive immediately, Beauregard might be overrun.

Johnston's command consisted of four infantry brigades and two cavalry regiments, with an artillery battery attached to each brigade. General Bernard Bee commanded a brigade from Alabama, Mississippi and Tennessee, Colonel Francis Bartow led a brigade from Georgia and Kentucky and Colonel Arnold Elzey commanded a brigade from Maryland, Tennessee and Virginia. Jackson's brigade, which led Johnston's departure from Winchester, included the Second, Fourth, Fifth, Twenty-seventh and Thirty-third Virginia, all of whom were from the Shenandoah Valley.

None of the soldiers in the ranks and few of the officers knew their destination as they marched through Winchester, and many of the townspeople thought that they were being deserted. Most of the soldiers, particularly in Jackson's command, agreed with them. With two Union armies threatening the town from the north and west, only a few hundred militia were left to defend the town. The students from Washington College in Lexington, Virginia—who were now part of the Fourth Virginia Infantry of Jackson's brigade and had been the particular focus of the girls in Winchester—felt disgraced to be marching away. Even officers of Jackson's staff were dismayed by the move. Major Frank Jones of Jackson's staff commented that the move caused "great dissatisfaction amongst those who came from the Valley."

Despite this, the people of the town cheered them wildly as they marched through downtown. Cornelia McDonald observed that the townspeople lined the streets, with "banners waving, the bands playing, and the bayonets gleaming in the noonday sun." Kate Sperry, who watched all of her new romantic interests march past her home, lamented that "she would die of boredom." Some of the more astute civilians began to suspect that something big was about to happen when the marching columns turned east onto the Millwood Pike. They were not heading south in retreat but in the direction where everyone expected the decisive battle of the war to take place.

An eerie silence fell over the town as the last soldiers disappeared from view. Although there were still plenty of sick soldiers to keep them busy, something was up and everyone knew it. Rumors began to circulate around town early on the morning of July 22. A horrific battle had been fought, and word of deaths among local soldiers began to disseminate through town. Chase heard that popular young attorney Lewis T. Moore, who lived close to her, had been killed and that one of the regiments had been "cut to pieces."

The next day, she learned to her relief that Moore had only been wounded but that "this has been a sad day to many hearts in this vicinity." Others worried about their own husbands, boyfriends or sons as the day wore on.

Later that day, word came that a great victory had been won at Manassas, but the joy of this triumph was quickly tempered when the cost of that victory also began to appear. Wagon trains began to arrive with the wounded; when the last one finally arrived, it carried the bodies of five members of the Winchester Rifles who had died in the battle. All of the stores on Loudoun Street closed in tribute to the fallen as the bodies of Lloyd Powell, Charles Mitchell, Isaac Glaize, William Young and Edward Burgess were returned to their grief-stricken families.

Robert Y. Conrad, who had fought so hard to avoid the war, was informed that his two nephews, Holmes and Tucker Conrad, were among the slain. They had been killed together. The news of their deaths was the first that their devastated father had heard of them since they enlisted. Others had cheated death by the closest of margins. Randolph and Strother Barton had been wounded, and their brother-in-law, Thomas Marshall, had his horse shot out from under him.

What was not readily known at the time was the part that Winchester's sons had played in the battle. Jackson, shortly after the battle, wrote to his wife about Henry House Hill, where his brigade fought; he stated that it was "to our army what the Imperial Guard was to the First Napoleon" and that "it met the thus far victorious enemy and turned the fortunes of the day." During the most critical part of the fight for Henry House Hill, General Bernard Bee, in a desperate attempt to rally his broken brigade, pointed to Jackson's brigade and yelled, "There stands Jackson like a stone wall, rally around the Virginians."

After the victory, stories of heroic stands, the capture of a Union battery and bayonet charges by Jackson's brigade spread like wildfire throughout the Confederacy. The young men who had marched off to war from Winchester to the cheers of their neighbors as members of the Winchester Rifles, Marion Rifles, Morgan Continental Guard and Mountain Rangers had earned a new nickname on the plains of Manassas. From that point forward, they would be known as the "Stonewall Brigade."

Chapter 3

"The Men Are in the Army"

As July turned into August in 1861, Winchester established an identity that continued throughout the war as a hospital center for wounded and sick soldiers from both sides. Although Richmond and Washington, D.C., housed many more injured and sick soldiers than the Valley town, both were much larger and had more facilities. With a population of a little over four thousand, a great number of whom were away in the army, Winchester was not prepared for this role and suffered for it. Churches, hotels, schools and warehouses were converted into hospitals in an attempt to meet the demand, and few private homes escaped the war without housing casualties; many backyards became impromptu cemeteries for the dead.

While the town struggled to cope with its losses at Manassas and care for the wounded and sick, another problem arose that both frightened and annoyed the citizens. With Johnston's army away at Manassas, the town's defenses against a Union occupation were reduced to several hundred militia who were stationed in the town, and most of these units were commanded by men with no military experience. In addition to being vulnerable to attack, poor regard to sanitation in camps in addition to a lack of discipline compounded the problem. An influx of soldiers, either sick, injured or healthy, taxed the town's resources to the breaking point. Providing food and shelter to so many drove prices up while also making life difficult and causing law enforcement problems.

Militia officers were almost always poor disciplinarians, and problems arose ranging from the annoying to the truly criminal. Gambling, drunkenness and

Above: First Maryland Infantry members playing football on the Frederick County fairgrounds. *GQ/BR*.

Left: Kate Sperry, the Rebel Winchester diarist who was courted by many Confederate soldiers during the war. *WFCHS*.

prostitution always followed any army, and the one in Winchester was no different. With little help from the militia officers, who seemed more inclined to participate in than check these activities, Winchester lacked enough police officers or sheriffs to cope with the problem. To make matters worse, two Union armies lay within easy marching distance of the town, and it was painfully obvious that the local militia units were no match for even a small raiding party.

The arrival of so many strangers, however, did bring its share of interesting characters. One was Belle Boyd of Martinsburg, perhaps the most notorious of the many female Confederate spies and one of the most active in the Shenandoah Valley. She was a regular visitor to Winchester, whether it was occupied by Union or Confederate forces, and was noted for more than her abilities in espionage, as Kate Sperry so aptly described her in her diary shortly after the Battle at Manassas:

> *Bell Boyd of Martinsburg, called this afternoon, and of all fools I ever saw of the womenkind, she certainly beat all—Perfectly insane on the subject of men—dark green riding dress with brass buttons down the front, a pair of Lieut. Col.'s shoulder straps—a small riding hat with a row of brass buttons on the rim from every state in the Confederacy—a gold palmetto breast pin and a real genuine palmetto stuck straight on top of her head—no brains—and you have a full picture of the farfamed Bell Boyd. She is the fastest girl in Virginia or anywhere else for that matter. Since the army has been around, her senses are perfectly gone—she is just from Centerville where the army is now—staid there a week and what with her staffs, Cols., Generals, Lieuts., etc., she is entirely crazy.*

Sperry, at this stage of the war, seemed to find almost everything about the new Confederacy fascinating or humorous. Most of the townspeople, however, found little interesting about Boyd or any other new arrival in town. With rising prices, increased crime and the need to care for large numbers of wounded and sick soldiers, the town's leaders began to petition Richmond for aid. When Colonel Angus McDonald's cavalry force was handily defeated near Romney, real fear of a Union occupation increased tensions. The only bright spot in this defeat was that the obviously incompetent McDonald was replaced by Turner Ashby, who proved to be one of the best cavalry officers of the war.

That, however, was in the future. What the town desperately needed was a force large enough to protect it and competent leaders. Robert Y. Conrad, along with several other notable citizens, wrote to General Jackson that the town was suffering "from the army under your command" and complained of "seven or eight thousand sick and straggling soldiers." The healthy soldiers were described as "loafing, disorganized" and "had for some time become a great nuisance."

The real problem, though, was that after the defeat at Manassas, President Abraham Lincoln was even more committed to winning the war. McDowell and Patterson were replaced by more energetic commanders. General George B. McClellan was brought from West Virginia to take command of the Union army around Washington, D.C., and was assembling a force of well over 100,000 men. In the Valley, General Nathaniel Banks replaced Patterson and was quickly organizing more than 30,000 soldiers just across the Potomac River from Virginia. In addition to that, the Union forces who had beaten McDonald and occupied Romney were less than fifty miles west of Winchester.

General Johnston at Manassas, who had about fifty thousand men to meet all of these threats, had few men to spare. Everyone, however, agreed that the Shenandoah Valley was vital to the survival of Virginia and had to be defended. With manpower in short supply, Johnston and the authorities in Richmond decided to send an officer with a reputation for discipline who would also appease the frightened Valley citizenry. Instead of sending any reinforcements, they sent newly promoted Major General Thomas J. Jackson.

It was an excellent choice for several reasons, not the least of which was the general's new nickname. After the Battle of Manassas, Jackson was now universally known as "Stonewall" Jackson. Despite his protest that the nickname belonged to his brigade and not to him, it stuck. He was also a citizen of the Valley, having lived in Lexington, Virginia, for about ten years before the war began, and his performance before Manassas with Valley soldiers was also well known and unanimously applauded.

The effect of Jackson's appointment was immediate. Conrad wrote to his son Holmes that "[t]he return here of Gen'l Jackson has had a great effect upon the spirits of our citizens" and that his assignment to Winchester "inspired confidence in our safety, and the loafing disorganized soldiery who had for sometime become a great nuisance among us, have disappeared from our streets."

After an emotional farewell to his brigade, Jackson left immediately for Winchester, accompanied by only two staff officers. The rest resigned out of respect for Jackson's new rank and command. With his responsibilities greatly increased, they believed that it was appropriate for Jackson to select whomever he wanted for his new command, now designated the Valley

The Lieutenant Colonel Lewis T. Moore House, used by Stonewall Jackson as his headquarters between November 1861 and March 1862. *GQ/BR.*

District. One of those who resigned was Frank Jones, but he was not without a position for long. The Frederick County native was quickly appointed major of the Second Virginia Infantry.

Arriving in the middle of the night on November 4, 1861, the new district commander established his headquarters at the Taylor Hotel. Shortly afterward, Jackson moved his permanent headquarters to the home of Colonel Lewis T. Moore on Braddock Street. Moore, who was severely wounded at the Battle of Manassas, was recuperating in Richmond and generously offered his vacant home to Jackson. (Moore's home is now a museum run by the Winchester–Frederick County Historical Society. He is also the great-grandfather of actress Mary Tyler Moore.)

Jackson immediately discovered that he was a commander without a command. With two sizable Union forces massing against him from the north and west, he had barely two thousand infantry and cavalry, most of whom had either antiquated weapons or none at all, and no artillery. Colonel Ashby's five-hundred-man cavalry force had proven to be excellent scouts, and the young colonel was universally admired by everyone. The rest of Jackson's command could only be described as a poorly armed, disorganized mob.

Having anticipated this, Jackson was lobbying for reinforcements before he left Johnston's army. The day after he arrived in Winchester, his old brigade and the Rockbridge Artillery were ordered to join him there. The delight over being ordered home was overwhelming for the officers and enlisted men of the brigade. Unfortunately, their enthusiasm was tempered liberally by alcohol during their journey from Manassas to Winchester. When the train from Manassas arrived at Strasburg, very few members of the brigade were sober.

The twenty-mile march north to Winchester and the hangovers many were suffering, however, did little to diminish their eagerness to see friends and loved ones. It was only toned down slightly when Jackson ordered them to camp several miles below town and then moved them north of town a few days later. Always the disciplinarian, he issued orders that no one, neither officers nor enlisted men, was to enter town without a pass. Despite these restrictions, the townspeople were equally overjoyed to have their loved ones near home and unanimously approved of the return of the Stonewall Brigade. Julia Chase recorded in her diary on November 9: "Our town is all astir in consequence of the arrival of Jackson's Brigade. The citizens of Winchester feel perfectly safe now, I suppose."

Jackson's orders against not entering town without a pass were generally ignored, and an almost continuous game of cat and mouse existed between members of the brigade and the hapless militia who guarded the town. On the same day, Chase noted that confrontations between the militia guards and members of the brigade began almost immediately after they arrived. It became a running battle that Jackson and his militia sentries seldom won.

The reunions, although joyous, proved brief. Jackson was committed to taking the offensive, believing that it was the only way to protect the Valley. According to his wife, Mary Anna, he felt that "a protracted struggle would wear the South out," and "[h]e believed that we had but one hope, and that was to press the Federals at every point, blindly, furiously, madly." Most Confederate leaders disagreed and wanted to simply defend their homeland, and they had little enthusiasm for offensive war. Jackson, while at Manassas, strongly advocated just the opposite, and many hoped that his assignment to Winchester would keep him too busy to advocate his views to his superiors. They were very much mistaken, though.

Jackson immediately began planning offensive operations that would keep his small army busy for the next eight months and eventually make legends of both Jackson and his soldiers. Convinced that standing on the defensive at Winchester was nearly impossible with his small force, Jackson began taking the offensive within a month of taking command. His primary interest

Kent Street Presbyterian Church. Stonewall Jackson attended this church while he was in Winchester, Virginia. *GQ/BR.*

was Romney, just fifty miles west of Winchester. The town, after Colonel McDonald's defeat, was occupied by a Union force who posed a continuous threat to the Lower Shenandoah Valley. Retaking West Virginia was also close to his heart since he grew up there.

With approval for an expedition to Romney delayed, Jackson launched two attacks on Dam No. 5 on the Chesapeake and Ohio Canal near Williamsport, Maryland. He hoped to seriously reduce, if not stop altogether, the supply of coal from western Virginia to the East Coast via the canal. Both expeditions, which his soldiers derisively referred to as that "Dam Expedition," proved unsuccessful. Jackson, however, was more determined than ever to launch an attack on Romney.

Despite Jackson's persistent attempts to take the war to the enemy, there was time for other activities while he was in Winchester. On December 21, his wife, Mary Anna, arrived at the Taylor Hotel. The deeply religious general had become a regular attendant at the Kent Street Presbyterian Church and had become close friends with its pastor, Reverend James Graham. Jackson arranged for his wife to stay with the Grahams, who only lived a short distance south of the Moore house on Braddock Street. The Grahams, who were close to the Jacksons in age, were happy to oblige, beginning a friendship that lasted for almost sixty years.

James Graham, pastor of Kent Street Presbyterian Church. *GQ/BR.*

Although held in very high regard professionally in town, Jackson and his wife's friendship with the Grahams helped open up doors for the couple socially. Graham's wife, Fanny, was the daughter of Anne Tucker Magill, who lived just a block away from the Kent Street Presbyterian manse on Braddock Street, where Mary Anna was staying with the Grahams. Magill, a widow, lived on Loudoun Street with her four daughters, who were very close to Mary Anna's age. The family matriarch, who was known for her great wit, must have made a lasting impression on "Stonewall." He told Mary Anna that he hoped she would be like Mrs. Magill when she reached advanced age.

Mary Anna also became close to Elizabeth Conrad, the wife of Robert Y. Conrad, whom she described as a gracious lady who "being foremost in all good works, in the hospitals ministering to the soldiers—and wherever they went their lives were devoted to the relief of suffering." Although all of the male Conrad children were in the army, the couple had two daughters at home. One of them, Sallie, was quite beautiful and had attracted the attention of several soldiers in town, including Henry Kyd Douglas (of Jackson's staff), who was deeply smitten with her.

The Kent Street Presbyterian manse on Braddock Street. Stonewall and Mrs. Jackson stayed at this house during the first three months of 1862; the Grahams are standing in front of the house in this picture. *GQ/BR.*

Another family with whom the Jacksons spent considerable time was that of Dr. Hugh McGuire, founder of the Winchester Medical College. The family also lived close by on Braddock, and the Jacksons took meals with them on a regular basis. Dr. McGuire's son, Hunter, was Jackson's personal physician and served as the medical director of the Second Corps of the Army of Northern Virginia when Jackson later commanded it. It was while dining with the McGuires that one of the most interesting events of Jackson's time in Winchester took place.

During the fall of 1862, Jackson and the Grahams were dining with the McGuires when their daughter, Gettie McGuire, asked the general for a photograph. Jackson immediately agreed and, with Reverend Graham, walked to the Loudoun Street studio of photographer Nathanial Routzann. When Routzann noticed that the general was missing a button on his uniform, Jackson asked for a needle and thread and sewed it on himself. The resulting photograph, with clear evidence of Jackson's lack of skill as a seamster, became Mary Anna's favorite.

Although Jackson generally attended Kent Street Presbyterian Church, Kate Sperry recorded at least one occasion when he attended Loudoun

General Stonewall Jackson. This picture was taken in Winchester, Virginia, by Nathanial Routzann in the fall of 1862 at the urging of Dr. Hunter McGuire's daughter, Gettie. *GQ/BR.*

Loudoun Street Presbyterian Church, where Julia Chase and her family attended church. *GQ/BR.*

Street Presbyterian Church, where Andrew Boyd was minister and Unionist Julia Chase and her family were members. Sperry, who could never resist the opportunity to size up the men in her presence, noted that Jackson, who led the congregation in prayer, was "right nice looking." She also commented that the church was "crowded and by way of enlivening the crowd and for the especial edification of said church a young lady, by the name of Josephine Singleton, concluded to have a fit."

Life, however, was not all church services, dinners and socializing for the man responsible for the protection of Winchester. Jackson's plan for an attack on Romney was finally approved. He was also provided with reinforcements for the expedition from General William W. Loring's brigade in southwestern Virginia, doubling the size of his small army. Jackson not only believed that a campaign against Romney would secure that part of the state for the Confederacy but also that a winter campaign was more likely to reduce the sickness that was prevalent in his army.

In both instances, he was completely wrong, and the Romney campaign proved to be one of the low points in his military career. Although Jackson did temporarily capture Romney, the effects on his army were disastrous. Marching and fighting in extremely severe winter conditions adversely affected his army to such an extent that thousands of soldiers either broke down, became seriously ill or deserted. Jackson's popularity, even within his own brigade, sank to an all-time low. Only the citizens of Winchester seemed to continue to have faith in him.

It is impossible to know for certain just how many soldiers were harmfully affected by the campaign. Various estimates generally agree that the number of sick and broken-down soldiers was enormous considering the size of his army. Julia Chase commented, "We have 1,800 sick in town and deaths are occurring every day. More die from exposure and sickness than are killed on the battlefield." Robert Y. Conrad, who believed that the figures were even higher, stated, "From three to four thousand are now here on the sick list." He added that "many have gone off home, and those left are unfit for the field." Even Dr. Hunter McGuire, Jackson's medical director, was unsure "how many men were sent back during the expedition."

When Jackson ordered Loring's brigade to remain at Romney while the Stonewall Brigade—which Loring's men referred to as "Jackson's pet lambs"—was sent back to Winchester, Loring and his regimental commander protested to Confederate authorities in Richmond. When Secretary of War Judah P. Benjamin went over Jackson's head and ordered Loring's brigade back to Winchester, Jackson promptly complied and then resigned.

Although he eventually withdrew his resignation, it took the efforts of several of his friends to persuade him. Even with Jackson still in command, serious damage to the effectiveness of his command had occurred and would have grave consequences as winter turned to spring.

With the arrival of spring, Banks's Union army of nearly 30,000 began slowly approaching Winchester. Jackson had barely 3,500 men to oppose him. Winchester, which was difficult enough to defend with equal numbers, was now in serious danger of what the townspeople feared the most: Union occupation. With Banks's army just a few miles north of town at Bunker Hill, Jackson was faced with fighting a battle against overwhelming odds or evacuating the town. On March 3, Jackson's army began to retreat south toward Strasburg. The effect on Winchester was immediate. Kate McVicar observed that "the gleam and glitter, the glory and romance of war seemed to die."

Winchester, which had offered its sons and husbands, cared for the wounded and sick, suffered through epidemics that had taken many of their family members and fed and housed Confederate soldiers, was now about to experience something that no one could have imagined just a few months before. For the first of what turned out to be more than seventy times, Winchester was about to change hands.

Chapter 4

"The Women Are the Devil"

Since the election of Abraham Lincoln in November 1860, tensions in Winchester had always existed between those who supported secession and those who opposed it. Those tensions had, at times, turned ugly, and with Confederate evacuation imminent, they took a decided turn for the worse. The obvious pleasure that the small Unionist community showed for their likely "liberation" by Banks's army infuriated the Confederates in town. Some even called for them to be shot.

Prominent Unionists were arrested and forcibly sent south. Jackson, fearing a security breach, arrested several after a Union meeting on March 10. That very day, Julia Chase wrote in her diary: "We are expecting nothing else but Father will be arrested, as we learned the secessionists have 150 names of the Union people." Although the number was actually only twenty, her fears for her ailing father were well placed. He was arrested the next day and sent to Strasburg. For Chase, it was the beginning of a long agony that would eventually cost her father his life. Harriet Griffith and her family fared only slightly better. She recorded that "Father started to go to there" but "[w]as told they had taken up more Union men and taken them on to Richmond." Hearing this, Harriet's father quickly returned home and avoided arrest and deportation.

The arrested Unionists were not the only ones leaving town. Many Confederate sympathizers were packing up and heading south, too. Perhaps the most famous was a young girl attending Mr. and Mrs. Charles L. Powell's school across the street from the McGuires on Braddock Street. Mildred

General Nathaniel Banks, the first Union general to occupy Winchester. *GQ/BR.*

Lee, the daughter of General Robert E. Lee, hurried off to join her parents in Richmond just before the town's occupation by the Union army. Another evacuee, fifteen-year-old Emma Riely, left for Luray, Virginia, but returned later that year. Her recollections, written forty years later, graphically described life in the beleaguered town.

Most, however, stayed, and one became the most celebrated diarist of the war in Winchester, at least to historians. Mrs. Mary Greenhow Lee, a widow in her mid-forties and a neighbor of both the Bartons and the Conrads on Market Street, began her diary the day the Union army arrived. Decidedly Confederate, she was much less concerned with bachelor soldiers than younger diarists like Kate Sperry and Harriet Griffith, and although full of venom for all things Yankee, her diary is primarily focused on events and is very accurate.

Mrs. Lee, as she was commonly known around Winchester, was born to a prominent Richmond family on September 9, 1819, and could trace her family genealogy back to the earliest Virginia colonists. She moved to

Mrs. Mary Greenhow Lee, the most prolific of the Winchester diarists and a devoted Rebel. *GQ/BR.*

Winchester in 1843 to marry local lawyer Hugh Holmes Lee and remained there after his death in 1856. Living with her on Market Street were Laura and Antoninette Lee, the sisters of her late husband, as well as her sister-in-law's two children. Although not as extensive as Mrs. Lee's, Laura also kept a diary during the war. At least one other relative, at least by marriage, visited her home in Winchester during the war. Her half brother, Robert Greenhow Jr., was married, until his death, to the celebrated Confederate spy Rose Greenhow.

With Unionists despondent about arrests and deportations, and Mrs. Lee and her Confederate sympathizers either leaving or stoically awaiting their fates, Banks's army approached Winchester by inches. On March 11, with only Colonel Turner Ashby's cavalry left in town, their Union counterparts began entering Winchester from the north. Ashby, after a show of bravado on the downtown streets that only increased his legendary status among Confederates in the Valley, was the last Confederate soldier to leave Winchester.

On March 12, 1862, Union general Charles S. Hamilton's command marched into Winchester and was met at the northern end of town by Mayor John B.T. Reed and the city council. The local dignitaries surrendered the town and asked for protection of private property. For the people of Winchester, especially the Confederates, having the Union soldiers enter town to the tune of "John Brown's Body" was galling. All of the diarists commented on the event, each taking it in from her own unique perspective.

Kate Sperry observed that she "never saw as many faces where evil predominated." She also promised herself that "if our men ever do come back here there are some persons I'm going to point out who appeared very glad to see them." Cornelia McDonald, who was eating breakfast with her children when the Union army arrived, said, "I tried to be calm and quiet, but could not, and so got up and went outside the door." Returning to the table, she was "amused at the expression of humiliation on the small faces around me." One had "tears of anger," while another "looked savage enough to exterminate them if he had the power."

The Mrs. Mary Greenhow Lee House on Market Street. General John B. Gordon's wife attempted to rally Confederate soldiers retreating after the Third Battle of Winchester in the street in front of Mrs. Lee's home. *GQ/BR.*

Mrs. Lee lamented that "[a]ll is over and we are prisoners in our own houses" and that "[f]or about an hour, death-like stillness pervaded the town, and then music and some cheering." As Union troops marched in front of her house on Market Street, she was "glad to say, the doors and windows are all closed." She later admitted that "I am astonished at myself, that I have not a sensation of fear, when I first heard their hateful music, I felt depressed and abased, but it was but for a moment, and I remembered how thankful I was that Jackson had not risked a battle, and that our precious little army was safe."

Of course, Julia Chase and other Unionists responded quite differently. Chase wrote, "Glorious news. The Union army took possession of Winchester today, and the glorious old flag is waving over our town." She also injected that "[t]he Union, which since the war broke out was changed to ION, removing the U and N has within a few days replaced the letters, giving it its original name." Chase, however, was still upset over the seizure of her father: "How indignant I felt toward the whole town! To take an old

Reverend Benjamin Brooke, pastor of Market Street Methodist Church. *GQ/BR.*

man lying sick on the sofa is outrageous." Harriet Griffith noted, "Of course we waved and bid them welcome."

Reverend Benjamin Brooke, pastor of Market Street Methodist Church, watched the Union army enter town from the top of a local building and observed, "Banks entered Winchester at 9 a.m. in a most martial manner—riding in a carriage drawn by four white mules." He continued, "My little son Robert flung himself on the ground in a passion of boyish grief." When Brooke picked him up, he kept repeating, "Jackson's gone—Jackson's gone." After calming him down, Brooke heard his son comment, "'Why, they look like people, don't they?' No doubt that he had been told that the Federals were devils," Brooke said.

Banks immediately issued strict orders on how his soldiers were to conduct themselves. He restricted them to camp without passes, pledged to protect the property of local citizens and warned of severe punishment for anyone who violated these directives. He also assured the citizens that no arrests would be made based on loyalty to the Confederate States. His orders, however, were much easier written than implemented.

A career New England politician, Banks was a former speaker of the House of Representatives and governor of Massachusetts. Although popular with his men, he was totally uneducated in military arms. His ineffectiveness as a post commander exacerbated problems between the occupying army and the townspeople. One soldier expressed the general feelings of most Union soldiers occupying the town: "Notwithstanding the real or pretended Union feelings here, the absence of the young men, and the sneers and the remarks of the females and children, proved that the rebellious element is not crushed."

Oddly one of the first near victims of this attitude was the Unionist Harriet Griffith and her family. Shortly after the Union occupation, her father "came home as some of the Federals had gone to take possession of the factory." The building was locked up because "they thought we were secesh." When her father explained that they were Unionists and Quakers, everything changed: "[T]hey stayed for supper and were ashamed of their conduct afterward. The captain came and apologized for their behavior."

The meal must have been a good one because they "came to breakfast and after till twelve o'clock the table was set. Had the flag out of course." The near mistake by the Federal soldiers, fortunately, turned into a memory that Harriet would never forget: "[T]hey cut their buttons of their coats and gave them to me," and "the Boston band were serenading us. Oh, it was splendid and I shall never forget—no, never." It was not the last time the young, comely Quaker girl would attract the attention of Union soldiers in town, and like her philosophical opposite, Kate Sperry, it would end happily.

Confederate sympathizers, particularly the women, did everything in their power to make the Union soldiers in town feel unwelcome. Mrs. Lee commented, "I am delighted to hear that they are very much disappointed at their reception here and say they were never treated with such scorn as by the Winchester ladies." When Union general James Shields began boarding with the Magill family, Mrs. Lee remarked that Anne Tucker Magill's daughter, Mary, "allows her tongue full license and says all kinds of bitter sarcasm to Gen. S. She told him that if they killed all of the men of the South, the women would fight, and that when they were destroyed the dogs would bark at them."

When a United States flag was raised over an office in town, Kate Sperry proudly declared, "None of the girls in the neighborhood will walk under it, they got out in the mud round it and on the pavement again." She continued, "It makes them furious, the horrid cut-throats," and predicted that "they'll stretch it across the whole street." Cornelia McDonalds stated, "Those that are here make a great display of their finery, and the grandeur of their equipment, but the people take no notice of it. I meet the gorgeous officers every day in our hall, but I never raise my eyes."

Reverend Brooke was infuriated when "Federal Chaplains called to see me." After inviting them into his home, "the Rev. McRhea slipped into

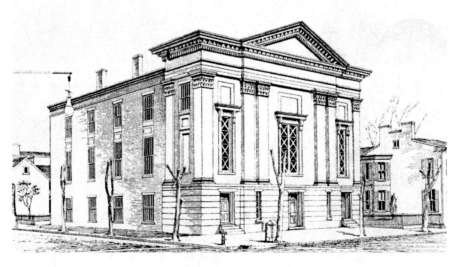

Market Street Methodist Church. *WFCHS.*

my kitchen and was trying to persuade my negro cook to run away." The next day, when Brooke entered his church to preach to his congregation, he "found it filled with soldiers—the Chaplains were there—Rhea was in the pulpit—he said that he was going to hold forth—and commenced with a hymn, and then such a prayer I never heard. 'Crush!, Crush!, Crush!' was his only idea."

Mrs. Lee would have been surprised to see so many Union soldiers in church. The very next Sunday, while attending church at Kent Street Presbyterian, she noticed that there were no Union soldiers in attendance. She derisively commented in her diary that Yankees were "not a church-going people." What Mrs. Lee and the rest of Winchester would soon realize was that on this particular Sunday morning, the Union soldiers had more pressing business to take care of than church: just south of town at the small hamlet of Kernstown, Jackson and his army had suddenly appeared.

Based on information provided by Colonel Ashby, whose cavalry continued to hover just south of Winchester, Jackson believed that the Union army had left and that only a small rear guard remained in town. The truth was that Banks had left with a division for Manassas with the idea of eventually reinforcing the large Union army advancing against the Confederate capital from the Virginia Peninsula, but an eight-thousand-man

General Turner Ashby, a legendary cavalryman who was buried in Winchester after the war. *GQ/BR.*

division under General Shields remained in Winchester and was double the size of Jackson's small force.

The ensuing Battle of Kernstown was observed from a distance by the excited townspeople. Reverend Brooke got his revenge for the invasion of his church that day—when observing the battle among a group of Union officers, he blurted out, "Oh, Lord, help Jackson." Although the officers ignored him, it is doubtful that they forgot his remark. The battle was a sharp, bloody affair and represented another agonizing stage in Winchester's introduction to war. Despite being fought with less than a sixth of the forces used at Manassas in July 1861, the casualties were just as great. This time Winchester would not be dealing with a few wounded or sick who accumulated gradually but rather with an instant infusion of several thousand severely wounded and dying soldiers from both sides. Jackson's defeat and retreat that evening began a harrowing experience that brought out the best in the town as wounded soldiers quickly filled up all of the public buildings, warehouses and churches.

Cornelia McDonald "[r]emained during all those miserable hours with my baby on my lap and four little ones clustered round." The next morning she witnessed "a worn and weary, ragged and hungry train of prisoners came in town under a strong guard." The Rebel prisoners were easily recognizable since many of them were the sons of local residents, including David and Fanny Barton, whose two sons had been captured in, of all places, Barton Woods near their country estate. McDonald surely spoke for everyone in town when she wrote, "No one knew who was dead, or who was lying out in that chilly rain, suffering and famishing for help that was so near."

The Union wounded and dying were brought in first, and McDonald, when entering one of the makeshift hospitals, saw that "[l]ong lines of blue clad forms lay on each side as I passed up the room." Carrying a pitcher of lemonade, she noticed a Union soldier who was so badly hurt he could not raise his head, "so I poured it into his mouth with a tablespoon." After he thanked her, she moved on to the other wounded. Later in the day, when she was leaving for home, "I saw them carrying his corpse towards the door."

McDonald's ordeal was only just beginning, though, as the Confederate wounded were finally brought into town: "I wanted to be useful, and tried my best, but at the sight of one face that the surgeon uncovered, telling me that it must be washed, I thought I should faint. As I passed my dress brushed against a pile of amputated limbs heaped up near the door. My faintness increased, and had to stop and lean against the wall."

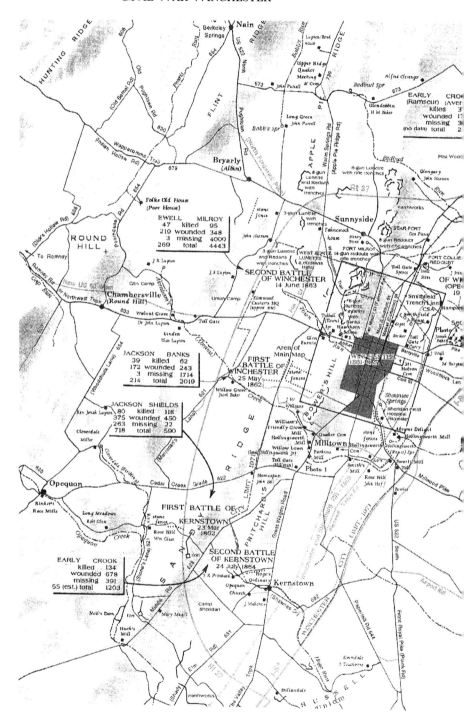

Frederick County, Virginia, drawn by Wilbur Johnston. *WFCHS.*

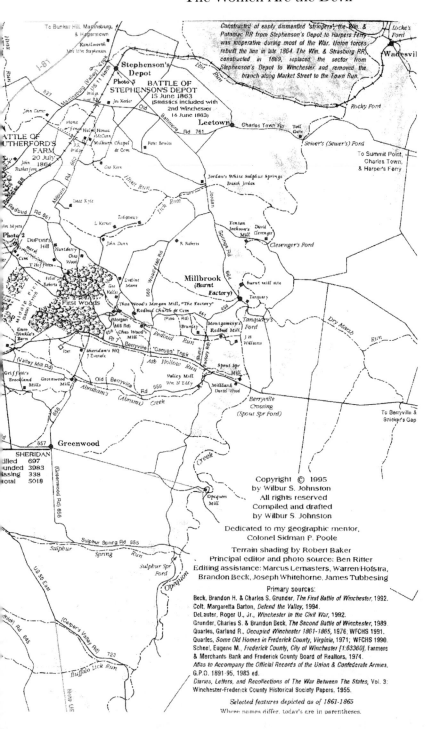

Coming to McDonald's rescue was the gregarious Anne Tucker Magill, mother of Reverend James Graham's wife:

Just then Mrs. Magill stopped by me on the way in, and asked what was the matter. I told her about the poor man whose wound I could not wash. "I'll wash him," she said, and with her sweet cheerful face she went in, and I saw her leaning over him as he laid propped up by a bench.

Another voice on the conditions after the battle came from the wife of a wounded Union officer. Mrs. Mary Kelly, after arriving in Winchester from Indiana, commented in a letter home, "This is a bad place for sick people. The wounded are dying every day. This is a three story building and very large at that and every room is full." She went on to add that "[t]he ladies here have been very kind to our men though there are plenty of Secesh here of the meanest kind."

Another visitor to town was William Seward, the secretary of state. Mrs. Lee proudly commented, "I must tell you Seward complimented us; when he returned to Washington. He was asked about Union feelings in Winchester, and his reply was, 'The men are all in the army and the women are the devil.'" She went on to add, "We hold our own bravely, you see."

Although Jackson's attack proved a failure tactically, it was a success in a strategic sense. Any thought of reducing the presence of Union forces in the Valley was now gone. A Confederate army in Winchester, which is geographically north of Washington, frightened Federal authorities, and Banks, with his division, was immediately returned to the Valley. Moving the majority of his forces south to Harrisonburg, he hoped to eventually drive Jackson from the Valley and capture the valuable railroad depot in Staunton. The wily Confederate commander, however, had other plans. Reinforced by a division under General Richard Ewell, Jackson began an aggressive campaign that quickly turned the tables in the Shenandoah Valley.

With the hard reality of battle now fresh in the minds of Union soldiers occupying Winchester, and Jackson's offensive threatening to remove them from the Valley, retaliation against those believed to be responsible for the bloodletting was initiated. With a large New England element within the Union army in the Valley, the retaliations were directed particularly against those favoring slavery.

Among these Union soldiers, there was little sympathy for a certain medical college in town that had used some of John Brown's raiders as cadavers. Although this fact was not discovered immediately, before Banks left Winchester the medical school, founded by Hunter McGuire's father, suffered a unique fate. On May 16, 1862, Mrs. Lee recorded: "In less than an hour there was another alarm and on opening the door the flames were ascending somewhat in the direction of Selma [the home of James Mason], but it proved to be the Medical College, which is burnt to the ground."

The next day, she stated, "The explanation of the burning of the college is that the skeleton of Oliver Brown [John's son] was there." However, she added, with some pleasure: "They buried in the yard what they supposed were his bones, but the genuine ones had been removed by Hunter McGuire, thus foiling their malicious designs." Whether Mrs. Lee was correct in assuming that young McGuire had spirited away any of the cadavers, the episode is still unusual. Despite being occupied by rival armies more than seventy times and witnessing nine battles within the county, the burning of the Winchester Medical College was the only recorded act of purposeful arson during the entire war in the town.

As Jackson's campaign progressed, news from the Upper Shenandoah Valley became more and more ominous. Unionists in town began to retreat back into anonymity as much as possible, and secessionists became bolder. On the morning of May 25, 1862, Winchester awakened to a stirring sound. Cannon fire and musketry could be unmistakably heard south of town, and Union soldiers were seen rushing about madly through the downtown streets. For the Confederates in town, it seemed like the answer to their most fervent prayers. Jackson was back, and this time he was coming with overwhelming numbers.

Chapter 5

"Oh Bess, What Visions of Glory Do Your Eyes Behold Now"

One of Winchester's leading citizens was Mrs. Betty Taylor Dandridge, who lived just a few blocks west of the McGuires on Boscawen Street. Dandridge, the daughter of President Zachary Taylor, was about to have a double thrill on the morning of May 25, 1862. Not only was she about to be reunited with her younger brother, Richard, but as the leader of the Louisiana Brigade of Jackson's army, he also played the decisive role in its victory that day. Launching a furious flank attack, Taylor's brigade sent Union soldiers running for their lives through downtown Winchester.

Perhaps the most unlikely soldier among the Confederates that day was the Bartons' fifth son, Robert. Considered sickly, he had attempted to enlist in June 1861, only to be rejected. Shortly before Jackson's evacuation in March 1862, he tried again, and this time the nineteen-year-old was accepted as a private in the Rockbridge Artillery. In his mess were two others with the same first name: Robert E. Lee Jr., the son of the general, and Bob McKim from Baltimore, Maryland. The battery nicknamed them the "Three Bobs," and the trio fought with the battery through the first phases of Jackson's famous Valley Campaign.

The assignment had the added benefit of putting Robert close to his brother, Marshall Barton, who was a lieutenant in the Jackson Light Artillery. While the two batteries were banging away at the Union position just south of town, tragedy struck twice. Shot through the neck, Marshall was killed during an artillery exchange, and the "Three Bobs" were reduced to two. In his memoirs, Robert recalled: "As we moved back to our proper positions,

Robert Barton. After repeated efforts to join and serve, he was eventually rejected for service in the Confederate army after Jackson's 1862 Valley Campaign because he was considered too weak and sickly. After the war, Barton became one of Winchester's most successful attorneys and was the author of several widely acclaimed law books. He died in 1917 at the age of seventy-four, outliving most of his contemporaries. *WFCHS.*

we passed the dead and wounded of our battery, and there lay Bob McKim dead, his fine and happy face stained with blood and his forehead crushed in by a bullet or fragment of shell."

As the Union line collapsed, there was no time to grieve for friends and loved ones as the Confederates chased the defeated Union army through the streets of Winchester. The scene in town was complete chaos. Cornelia Wilson, wife of Methodist minister Norval Wilson, in a letter to her brother said, "Mrs. Carsons says the balls rattled on her roof like hail" and that "[t]hey came through every street, over the hills, in every direction. The commons was filled with flying soldiers, dropping everything as they went."

Kate Sperry's next-door neighbor, Tillie Russell, could not resist the temptation to see what was going on. She "opened the front door, which is on Loudoun Street, and as she did so a Minnie ball struck a brick near her head." Despite nearly being killed, Russell threw open the door just as Taylor's brigade was running by. She was not alone. With bullets flying everywhere, hundreds of citizens entered the streets to cheer the Confederates. When Jackson rode through town, his welcome on Loudoun Street was something that few of them would ever forget. Cornelia McDonald in her diary recounted that "[p]eople from different spheres of life, who perhaps never before had exchanged a word, were shaking hands and weeping together."

What happened during this wild, chaotic clash was also a source of controversy that affected the treatment that the town received from the Union army for the rest of the war. Many Union soldiers claimed that while running through the streets of Winchester they were fired upon by civilians, especially women. A soldier in the Fifth Connecticut Infantry wrote to his father, saying that "[i]n many instances the young women were seen to fire revolvers from their houses." Although adamantly denied, at least twenty-four Union soldiers testified that they were fired upon by Winchester civilians during their escape through Winchester.

As Jackson's stunning victory swept the Union army before them, victory was accompanied by sorrow. McDonald wrote in her diary that while Fanny Barton was standing in her doorway passing out refreshment to the Confederates:

> [O]ne touched her and told her that her son, Marshall, had been shot not far from her home. Soon a squad of men came up with the body. He was already dead, shot in the neck. She led the way into her house, and directed them where to lay him. "He was born in that room and he shall lie there." Then all day she sat by him, wiping the blood that oozed from his wound.

The joyous citizens were unaware of the fact that while it was one thing for Jackson to drive the Union army out of Winchester, it was quite another to hold it for any length of time. Within days of his triumphal entry into the Valley town, Jackson and his army were forced to retreat, as two powerful Union armies drove into his rear. With Jackson's departure, another Union army arrived in Winchester less than two weeks after Jackson's victory.

As the Union army was humiliated by its recent defeat, and incensed by its treatment as it fled through the town after the battle, Winchester's life as a Union-occupied town was about to get a lot uglier, and even the Unionists were not immune. Several Quakers wrote after the war that when their meeting hall was used by Confederates as a hospital, "it was left in pretty good condition." But the day after the Union army arrived, "the Military authorities demanded the Key and took possession of the Meeting House. Friends never used it again. The entire fencing around the lot and a portion of the inside work of the Building were destroyed by Banks Army during the time he occupied Winchester."

By the end of the war, the Quakers' meetinghouse was so thoroughly destroyed that they were forced to build a new one. The town's African

American community was deprived of their church when the Union army used it as a storage facility for ammunition. Reverend Benjamin Brooke, who had prayed for Jackson during the Battle of Kernstown, may have been ignored by the Union officers at the time, but they had not forgotten. Brooke recorded in his journal on Sunday, June 15, 1862: "No church today—the building is so filthy. The Yankee soldiers used the choir gallery as a toilet the last day they were in it. What next!"

Although conditions in town were worse than ever, news from Jackson and his army was encouraging. After slipping by the two armies sent to trap him, Jackson turned just east of Harrisonburg and defeated both of them at the twin Battles of Cross Keys and Port Republic. Although the victories sent shock waves through the North, it also brought more heartache to Winchester. General Turner Ashby, who had won the heart of the Shenandoah Valley and the entire South, was killed near Harrisonburg on June 6, 1862.

Ashby, since the very beginning of the war, had endeared himself to the citizens of Winchester by his charismatic personality, his constant vigil at the picket posts, his heroic deeds and his commitment to their Valley. He led from the front and was generally where the fighting was most severe. Almost every young man in the Valley desired a place in his command, and his unexpected death shocked the entire community. Winchester never ceased to admire its favorite cavalier. His funeral in Winchester, shortly after the war, was the largest of its kind in the town's history, and both the local Sons of Confederate Veterans Camp and United Daughters of the Confederacy chapter are named in his honor.

Another casualty of the two battles was Robert Barton. The rigors of the campaigning proved too much for the frail youth. Spending most of the Battle of Port Republic in a ditch, unable to move from sheer exhaustion, Barton was discharged shortly after the battle and given a new assignment. Although not as exhaustive, it was probably equally dangerous. He spent the rest of the war searching for nitrate for gunpowder by crawling into caves and foundations of houses, both of which were the homes of a variety of poisonous reptiles.

Despite Jackson's success, there was no relief from Union occupation. The Valley army was needed in Richmond, where General George McClellan and his Army of the Potomac were at the door of the Confederate capital. The town went through several different commanders over the summer of 1862. After Banks, General Franz Sigel brought his German division to the embattled town. Many did not speak English, had no interest in the causes that started the war and were not inclined to show any compassion.

"Oh Bess, What Visions of Glory Do Your Eyes Behold Now"

Kate McVicar, known as "Nemo" when she wrote extensively of her Civil War experiences in the *Winchester Evening Star* thirty years later. *GQ/BR.*

Years after the war, Kate McVicar described the treatment of a friend at the hands of the Germans. One day, she went into the kitchen, "and two drunken Dutch soldiers came in clanking their sabers and flourishing their revolvers." Asked to leave, "one of them pointed his revolver at my breast." When she ran to her room and shut the door, "he tried to break it open, and failing, he raged around like a wild beast." Fortunately, several Union officers were nearby to rescue her.

McVicar's friend was not the only one to suffer as these foreign soldiers rampaged through the town, looting and stealing everything they could. L.E. Swartswelder's hardware store was looted, and six thousand cigars were stolen from Lloyd Logan's tobacco store. Roaming through town without supervision, the German soldiers broke down doors and demanded food or other items from helpless families.

Fortunately, Sigel and his German division's stay was brief, and Winchester, for a short time, returned to a quiet, if not happy, existence. Events near Richmond were altering conditions everywhere in Virginia. General Robert

Major Frank and Susan Jones. Major Jones's death after the Battle of Gaines' Mill left his widow with four small children, one of whom was not born until October, nearly four months after his death. *GQ/BR.*

E. Lee's army, with the addition of Jackson's Valley men, defeated McClellan in one of the bloodiest battles of the war thus far. Although pleased with the results, news from the battlefield was also accompanied by the loss of one of the town's most beloved citizens.

Major Frank Jones of the Second Virginia Infantry, suffering from diarrhea, was forced to participate in the Battle of Gaines' Mill on horseback. All three of the field grade officers of the regiment were either killed or wounded. Jones was wounded in the leg and spent the night on the battlefield in great pain. His leg was amputated at the field hospital the next day, and he was moved to a Richmond hospital on July 29. Although the wound was not necessarily fatal, the horrible conditions at the hospital and his weakened condition before the battle contributed to his death. The young major developed typhoid fever and died on July 9.

Jones's roots ran deep in the Shenandoah Valley. His great-grandfather, Gabriel Jones, was Lord Fairfax's lawyer and had overseen most of the legal issues concerning his 1.5-million-acre grant in northern Virginia. His mother, Ann Cary Randolph Jones, lived as a widow at her home, Vaucluse, near Middletown. Frank's sister was Fanny Barton, and his wife was Susan

Clark, whose brother, Peyton Clark, was the principal of the Winchester Academy and one of the most respected educators in the area.

Having just turned thirty-four, Jones left a wife and four children, one of whom would not be born until October 1862. Colonel William S.H. Baylor of the Fifth Virginia Infantry described Jones after the battle:

> *If there ever lived a pure man, he was Frank Jones. With almost everything that could be desired to make him a friend, he possessed that unpretending and yet ever noticeable piety which is the brightest and rarest of soldierly qualities, together with so much good sense and gentleness of manner that his influence was felt wherever he went.*

Decades later, grizzled Winchester veterans of some of the bloodiest battles ever fought in North America were brought to tears at the mere mention of his name.

The loss of Ashby and Jones within a few weeks was a serious blow to Winchester. With the Confederate victory at Richmond, conditions in the Valley town became much worse. Federal policy toward citizens under its control, for the most part, had been conciliatory. Most believed that the majority of Southerners opposed secession and would happily rejoin the Union if given the chance. The twin Confederate victories in the Shenandoah Valley and before Richmond, as well as the treatment given Union soldiers by towns like Winchester, left no doubt that secession had warm support from the majority of Virginians.

Federal policy became increasingly harsh as the Lincoln administration committed itself to preserving the Union at all costs. A new Union army, primarily made up of soldiers who had fought against Jackson in the Valley, was assembled near Culpeper under the command of General John Pope. The new commander warmly supported the harsher war measures, including denying essential items to citizens who supported the South. In order to obtain these necessities, citizens were now required to take a loyalty oath. Those who did not were threatened with arbitrary searches, denial of food and medicine and destruction of their property.

Fortunately, the new policies were not enforced with much zeal. What evolved was a system of "selective enforcement" that targeted community leaders, people whose actions were considered particularly obnoxious and those suspected of spying. Several leading citizens tried to negotiate a compromise, but one very important citizen refused. Robert Y. Conrad saw the loyalty oaths as a measure designed to treat civilians as prisoners of war. For his stance, he was promptly arrested and was charged with "being a disloyal citizen." After a heated argument with Union officials, he was released. When they threatened to search his home, he wrote to his son Holmes that he believed that "we have really fared better for maintaining a bold stand" and that "any attempt to invade my home would be met with such force as I could employ."

Although suspected of Union sentiments early in the war, Conrad quickly became one of the most important leaders (if not the most important) of civilian Confederates in Winchester. When he, along with Mayor Reed and Philip Williams, met later with Union authorities, they complained to them about their concerns regarding harsh treatment of Unionists in town and how many citizens were passing information to the Confederate army. In response, Conrad and his group issued a public statement that made clear that no one should be treated like criminals "on account of his opinions or sentiments" providing that they lived peacefully in their homes.

One Union measure ended humorously. While General Julius White was in command in Winchester, a homesick Emma Riely returned from her stay in Luray. Since mail delivery was uncertain in the Lower Shenandoah Valley, when someone was traveling to Winchester, they were asked to carry letters. Riely, who entered Winchester with several letters, was immediately detained by Union authorities. She was then subjected to a strip-search by Mrs. Delemesi, the wife of a Union officer. She recorded in her reminiscences: "Had she served an apprenticeship, she could not have been more thorough." Then Riely continued: "Corset stays were thoroughly examined, the shoes taken off, hands run down inside, but thank heavens they came up empty."

When the Confederate army occupied the town just a few weeks later, Mrs. Delemesi was caught behind Confederate lines. Fearing punishment, she refused to leave her boardinghouse. When Riely heard of her dilemma, she commented, "Don't ease her mind, please, for I want to punish her that way alone." Riely—the daughter of one of Winchester's most distinguished citizens and a member of the Kent Street Presbyterian Church, which was next door to her home—at fourteen, may not have been the oldest of the women who recorded their war experiences, but she may have been the most clever. Despite her strong Confederate leanings, she was not above using Union soldiers when it suited her purposes.

Winchester, like the rest of the Shenandoah Valley, was first and foremost a Christian community. The Valley was founded by religious dissenters, and each group took its beliefs seriously and, at least under the British Crown, suffered for it. Nothing, however, tested their religious faith like the Civil

Emma Riely, a Winchester teenager who was strip-searched for letters by Union authorities. *GQ/BR.*

War. Members of the same denomination spied on one another, snubbed one another and suffered indignities at the hands of Northern soldiers who worshiped in the same church with them. But even more damaging to their beliefs was the constant suffering that seemed so unfair.

One other common denominator was death. Very few families by the fall of 1862 had escaped without losing a member or a close friend. It was also difficult to witness the death and suffering of strangers, from both armies, who filled their hospitals. Cornelia McDonald's experience with the dying Union soldier after the Battle of Kernstown was a typical experience shared by almost all of the citizens of Winchester.

Enemy harassment paled compared to the strain of losing loved ones, particularly the very young. To make matters worse, the soldiers who entered town invariably brought disease with them that took the lives of small children and the elderly on a regular basis.

McDonald had suffered all of these woes except one. That, however, was about to change. On October 29, 1861, McDonald gave birth to a girl

Cornelia McDonald, a Winchester diarist who cared for seven children in Winchester during the Civil War. *GQ/BR.*

whom she named Elizabeth. Her diary clearly reflects the love and devotion she had for this new family member, whom she called "Bessie" for short. Bessie was her anchor through the gathering storm that was sweeping everyone in town. Hardly a day passed that she did not mention her in her diary, as well as how the young baby's eyes followed her wherever she went. Unexpectedly, Bessie became ill. On July 10, 1862, McDonald recorded in her diary: "My little darling Bessie was restless in her crib. I heard upstairs fretting, and went up stairs and saw her sitting up in her crib with one little hand holding to the bar, and the moon shining full on her."

With Winchester full of dying and wounded soldiers, doctors had no time to treat Bessie's illness. With medical care nonexistent, it is little wonder that McDonald's July 10 diary entry was her last for fifteen days. She recorded one more entry on the twenty-eighth, and then there is silence for two months. Finally, on September 26, she began:

Oh! The sorrow they have left me. They have taken away my flower. My sweet blue-eyed baby has left me forever. Though for many nights I have set with her in my arms soothing her restlessness, the day time would come and bring smiles and happy looks, and I had not a thought of dangers. One evening as the sun was going down I held her in my arms, and as she breathed out her little life her eyes were fixed on my face with the shadow of death over them. The children stood around sobbing. The little breast heaved and panted, a long sigh and all was still; her eyes stilled fixed on my face.

As Cornelia McDonald stood stunned and overwhelmed with grief, her young daughter-in-law, Betty, blurted out, "Oh Bess, what visions of glory do your eyes behold now."

Chapter 6

"We Looked to Him and Him Alone"

With the twin victories by Confederate armies in the Shenandoah Valley and around Richmond, Winchester's role in the Civil War was changing, and the town was adapting as best it could. Robert E. Lee's army followed these victories with a lightning advance to the Potomac River and beyond. After his victory in late August 1862 against General John Pope's Union army at Manassas, Lee moved his army into Maryland. These battles also exposed something that no one had anticipated when the war began. Almost everyone, North and South, expected the war to be short, and no one expected the enormous casualties it brought. The First Battle of Manassas, which had barely five thousand casualties on both sides, was followed in April 1862 by the Battle of Shiloh, which in two days resulted in twenty-five thousand casualties, more than twice the number for the entire Revolutionary War.

The battles Lee was fighting in Virginia were even bloodier. Beginning with a force of about ninety thousand men in mid-June, the Confederate army entered Maryland with a little over forty thousand. Although the battle casualties were staggering, many more soldiers, like Robert Barton, were completely broken down by the rigors of marching, fighting and living on poor rations. With Lee in Maryland, Winchester became a holding center for thousands of Confederate soldiers who were still game to fight but were in no physical condition to keep up with the army.

Winchester's role in revitalizing the Confederate army during this period was, perhaps, its greatest contribution to the war effort. After the Battle of Antietam in mid-September, which was the bloodiest day of the war,

Winchester was overwhelmed with Confederate wounded from that battle, too. Soldiers from as far away Texas, Arkansas and Florida were recovering and dying in this Shenandoah Valley town. The measure of the town's success was that by December Lee's army was able to fight the Battle of Fredericksburg with more than eighty thousand soldiers. The quick recovery of Lee's army was due, in large part, to the women of Winchester.

The influx of all of these broken-down soldiers was something new for Winchester. Mrs. Lee commented that "there must be 5,000 here," probably an understatement. She went on to complain that she would "rather have the advance than the refuse of our army." Robert Y. Conrad complained that the town was full of the "[s]ick—ragged—Skulking—begging—and etc." Food was running out, and the town would suffer another series of epidemics. There were also still many wounded from Jackson's Valley Campaign, and in late September there were added several thousand more from Antietam.

Ann Cary Randolph Jones, the mother of Major Frank Jones and Mrs. David W. Barton and the grandmother of Fanny Barton. *WFCHS.*

"We Looked to Him and Him Alone"

Julia Chase recorded on September 15: "Our town is filled with soldiers, and every house almost contains them. The pavements and cellar doors are lined with them—great many are disabled troops not fit for much duty." Kate Sperry's diary, unlike a year before, has little about flirting with prospective beaus or entertaining young soldiers in her home. She was too busy with the daily task of carrying food to York Hospital, Market Street Methodist Church, the Union Hotel and several hospitals (she was unsure whether they had names or not). Major Frank Jones's mother, Ann C.R. Jones, could not believe "the number of wounded that have passed through & remaining in Winchester."

Several buildings had been converted into hospitals since the Battle of Kernstown in March 1862. Almost all of the churches were used, but hotels, schools, warehouses and finally people's homes were also pressed into service to care for the latest sick and wounded. There was almost no home in Winchester or Frederick County that was not used as a hospital at some point during the war. A few of these stays did prove to be enjoyable, though. One soldier, after recovering from a wound at the home of John H.S. Funk's parents, commented that his sister Mollie was "a very lovely character."

Despite short supplies and inflationary prices, the women of Winchester provided meals for wounded soldiers. Even the most ardent Southern sympathizers in town never showed favoritism to these suffering and dying men based on the color of their uniform. Many a Union soldier was treated to a home-cooked meal by the mother, wife or daughter of a Confederate soldier. It was difficult even for the most hardened follower of the blue or the gray not to have sympathy for the helpless on both sides.

Conrad's wife, Elizabeth, a regular visitor to the hospitals, was surprised that the Confederate wounded "were on very friendly terms with the Yankees" and added that they "kill each other on the battlefield and share delicacies in a hospital." The Frederick County Courthouse, which was used as a temporary prison for captured soldiers, as well as a hospital, was the victim of the desire of some soldiers to vent. After the war, the walls were found to be covered with graffiti that can still be seen today. A more serious reminder of Winchester's role as a medical center for Civil War wounded is visible inside a building once used by Colonel George Washington during the French and Indian War, where bloodstains are still visible on the floor.

One of the most important innovations in medical care took place in Winchester during this period, thanks in large part to native son Dr. Hunter

McGuire. After Stonewall Jackson captured Winchester in May 1862, he discovered three surgeons and four assistant surgeons from the Union army caring for their soldiers from Banks's army. Normally, surgeons were treated as prisoners of war and imprisoned until exchanged. McGuire thought that this was a cruel waste of qualified doctors who were desperately needed by both armies.

Approaching Jackson on the subject, he suggested enemy surgeons be unconditionally released so that they could care for the wounded, wherever the surgeons found them. Jackson agreed, and McGuire put this agreement in writing and asked the Union surgeons to go to Washington and secure an agreement with the Federal government to make this the policy for all surgeons during the war. Released to travel to Washington, the Union surgeons persuaded Secretary of War Edwin Stanton to consent to the agreement, and it became policy for both armies for the rest of the war.

Dr. Hunter McGuire, Winchester native who was Stonewall Jackson's personal physician. *WFCHS*

"We Looked to Him and Him Alone"

Dr. Hunter McGuire's boyhood home on Braddock Street. *GQ/BR.*

With Lee's withdrawal from Maryland, the survivors of the bloody Battle of Antietam were added to the huge number of soldiers in the area. Camped north of town near the hamlet of Bunker Hill, the arrival of the entire Army of Northern Virginia put many soldiers in proximity with their loved ones. Unfortunately, few were able to spend any time with their families primarily because of the poor condition of both the army and the town.

With the army's deteriorated condition, disease was rampant among them. Few Winchester townspeople were willing to be exposed to more sickness, even if it meant not seeing their loved ones. When General D.H. Hill discovered some cases of smallpox in his division, both the townspeople and the army were in complete agreement that the two should remain separated. One of the few people who may have had some communication with the army was Kate Sperry. Although she thought he was "much too good" for her, Dr. Enoch Hunt of the Second Mississippi Infantry apparently disagreed and had been writing her since he left for Manassas with General Johnston's army in June 1861. The two were probably able to spend some time with each other since he was working at one of the hospitals.

Another change was the dramatic transformation in the young men from Winchester who had been shopkeepers, laborers and farmers. Dr. John Henry Funk, who enlisted as a private in the Fifth Virginia Infantry in April

81

1861, had risen to the rank of colonel in a little over a year and was now the commander of his regiment; he also served briefly as Winchester's provost marshal in September 1862. Funk's rapid rise was unusual but not unknown in Lee's army.

For the local men still in the ranks, gone was the youthful enthusiasm of 1861, the brightly colored homemade uniforms were now thread-worn rags and the trunks and baggage were gone and replaced with only what they could carry. They had evolved into grizzled veterans who had seen more death and suffering in a year and a half than most would see in three lifetimes, and they had proven themselves superb soldiers in some of the most difficult battles and maneuvers in American military history. Jackson's command, now the Second Corps of the Army of Northern Virginia, was collectively known as the "Foot Cavalry" for its reputation for rapid movements and was considered one of the elite organizations in either army. The cost for these achievements, however, was staggering. The Stonewall Brigade, which had fought the First Battle of Manassas with about 2,500 men, retreated from Maryland in September 1862 with fewer men than made up a single regiment just a year before. Many who were wounded would eventually return to duty, but just as many would not.

Lieutenant Colonel Lewis T. Moore, wounded at First Manassas, had ended his service to the Stonewall Brigade, and to that was added Colonel Frederick Holliday. Although quite young, Holliday had been considered one of the most promising lawyers in Winchester before the war. He had risen quickly to command the Thirty-third Virginia Infantry but was lost to the service when he was severely wounded at the Battle of Cedar Mountain in August 1862. Countless privates and noncommissioned officers would also never return to the ranks of the famed brigade.

Despite the victories and the revitalization of the Confederate army in October and November 1862, it was still impossible for it to hold Winchester whenever the Union army advanced. Most understood this and viewed the Confederate withdrawal in November with stoic pride. One Confederate soldier marveled at the town's goodbye:

> *Such an enthusiastic reception we never rec'd before. The streets and windows are thronged with men, women, and children almost frantic with delight to see their ragged grey rebels go by. Their deafening cheers, their excited gestures, their eager faces, all that we saw convinced us beyond all doubt that they were truly in earnest, and although we were*

leaving them to become again the helpless prey of an unfeeling and brutal foe, yet the very sight of our scarred and war torn victories so aroused their old Virginia spirit that all thought of self and their own loss seemed to be forgotten or merged in the great idea of our glory and the benefit of the whole country.

It was very hard, however, to say goodbye to one particular Confederate soldier. Stonewall Jackson had endeared himself to the town over the last year, and no one was happy when he departed. Mrs. Lee, who had not met Jackson until that fall, emotionally begged him while he was visiting her home "not to leave us" and assured him that "we looked to him and him alone" for our defense and safety. Jackson reassured her that if it were up to him, "Winchester would be his headquarters." Little did Mrs. Lee or anyone in the town know that this farewell would be the last time they would ever see their beloved "Stonewall."

The withdrawal of the Confederate army left Winchester fearful of what was next. For a brief time, no Union occupying force entered town, but the dread of its return dominated the people's thoughts. Mrs. Lee admitted that she feared "the raids of the Yankees far more than a permanent occupation." Fanny Graham, writing to Mrs. Jackson, stated that "[e]very time they come they are worse than before." Her words proved prophetic. Union occupation had evolved from conciliatory to harsh in 1862, and as 1863 dawned it would change again. This time it would be about vengeance.

The first Union commander to enter Winchester was General Gustaz P. Cluseret, but it was his replacement who had the most lasting impression on the town. On January 1, 1863, General Robert Milroy took command in Winchester. It was a stay that no one in town would ever forget. The Ohio abolitionist was determined, as he wrote his wife, to "play the tyrant among these traitors" and noted that "H___ is not full enough, there must be more of Secession women of Winchester to fill it up." Kate McVicar, years later, stated that "both Banks and White were Arch-Angels by the side of the unspeakable Milroy."

Milroy was as good as his word and immediately began making life miserable for the people of Winchester. One of his first steps was to require citizens to take a loyalty oath to the United States government or be denied many of the essentials of life. Passes in and out of Winchester were denied, many stores were not allowed to sell food and other supplies and, with winter in full force, firewood could not be purchased without the oath. It was obvious to everyone that Milroy's plan was to starve or freeze the women and children of Winchester into submission.

General Robert Milroy, the most hated of the Union generals who oversaw an occupation of Winchester. *GQ/BR.*

Not satisfied to just deny essentials for survival, the new Union commander employed a spy named Purdy to gather damaging information on those in town who held on loyally to their sons and husbands away in the Confederate army. Although few citizens had been forcefully removed from town because of their views since March 1862, Milroy used Purdy's espionage activities to gather information for the removal of those he held to be "disloyal." Mary Magill, Fanny Graham's sister, was thrown out of town for writing a letter to a friend in New Jersey about Milroy's policies. Andrew Boyd, Julia Chase's minister at the Loudoun Street Presbyterian Church, was arrested and sent to prison at Fort McHenry for a sermon he preached.

With the town suffering from a scarcity of almost everything, Milroy's policies threatened to add starvation to the long list of things that were killing the people of Winchester. One soldier, passing through Winchester shortly before Milroy's arrival, stated that the town was in "dreadful condition" and spoke about their "having scarcely any food, and being almost without means, and destitute of fuel for fire to cook their food."

Things reached the point of ludicrousness. Emma Riely related an incident that occurred in Milroy's office after he had banned the sale of feed to disloyal residents. According to Riely, when she went to Milroy's office, he was in a rage with Miss Arnold and blurted out, "You all brought on this devilish rebellion and ought to be crushed and starved with the cows." Arnold yelled back, "Well, General Milroy if you wish to crush this devilish rebellion by starving John Arnold's cow, you can do it and be drat." She then stormed out of his office.

The most memorable of Milroy's many acts against the town was one committed by his wife, whom Riely described as

> *a western women, from the backwoods evidently. Her hair was done up in the most antiquated style, parted and plastered down her face, making a sudden and violent curve to bring it back behind the ear, and ended in a little hard knot the size of a hickory nut. Her figure was in keeping, modeled after a block of wood, that same size all the way up.*

Mrs. Milroy had a great desire for the Logan House on Braddock Street and persuaded her husband to obtain it for her. Unlike John Arnold's cow, throwing the Logans out of their home was an outrage that the entire community, both Union and Confederate, noticed. Mrs. Logan and her children were thrown out of the house with nothing more than the clothes on their backs. Her furniture, her silverware and everything else of any value were stolen by the Milroys. Kate Sperry noted, "All of Mr. Logan and his sons clothing was confiscated, together with the house and furniture." Mrs. Milroy, Sperry said, "sat in an ambulance and viewed their removal with the utmost complacency. Old Milroy wouldn't let Mrs. Logan have a teaspoon to take her medicine out of—the old villain."

Another problem, if there were not enough already, was the complete breakdown of the town's infrastructure. With all of the buildings in use as hospitals, schools had been closed since the first Union occupation. Simple things like proper sanitation were neglected to the point that the town had become a giant wasteland of trash and refuse. Thirteen-year-old Gettie

The Lloyd Logan House on Braddock Street. *GQ/BR.*

Miller and her sister, Emma, who lived across the street from Sperry and were playmates with her sister, Jennie, prayed together each night for rain "to clean the streets."

In the midst of this, Winchester received the worst news imaginable. Although the news of another stunning victory by General Lee at Chancellorsville in early May caused jubilation, it was short-lived when the news arrived a few days later that Stonewall Jackson was dead. Mrs. Lee expressed her grief, and the town's, when she recorded that "all remembrance of the events of the day is obliterated by the calamitous rumors of this evening; the Richmond papers contain the obituary of Genl. Jackson. A gloom, still deeper, is over our town; the sad news is kept as far as possible out of hearing of the sick and fevered patients; men women and children weep for their hero."

Many of the town's women began wearing a badge of mourning for Jackson. Milroy forbade them and threatened expulsion for any caught wearing one. Even a black woman, who was caught wearing the badge, was not exempt and was removed from the town for her act of "disloyalty." The combination of Milroy and the loss of Jackson was almost too much for a town that had suffered greatly over the last two years. Facing starvation, imprisonment, the loss of property, the overwhelming task of caring for the wounded and sick, the loss of their most beloved hero and the threat of expulsion from the town by Milroy, it is little wonder that Winchester was near collapse. With all hope nearly gone and many resigned to their fate, into the breach stepped the most unlikely of heroes: the Union army.

Kate McVicar put it best in an article for the *Winchester Evening Star* several decades after the end of the war: "For one Milroy there were ten better men" in the Union army. While Milroy apparently did not understand the meaning of the word, his officers and enlisted men seemed to identify with the word "Union." It was, after all, what they were fighting for. At great danger to themselves, those who had risked their lives for that Union provided for the needs of the starving citizens of Winchester, whatever their political views. Exchanging coffee, vegetables and meat for fresh baked bread, the Union soldiers kept life at least bearable. Others turned a blind eye as people brought firewood or other supplies into town from the county.

General Richard Ewell.
GQ/BR.

Events from as far away as Mississippi, however, were about to affect Winchester. With Vicksburg under siege by a Union army and little help available, Confederate authorities decided to risk everything on another invasion of the North. Lee's army, heavily reinforced, was headed to Pennsylvania. In the van was Stonewall Jackson's Second Corps, now under the command of General Richard Ewell. With more at stake than ever before, Winchester was about to change hands again.

Chapter 7

"Can It Be Possible that We Are a Nation of Cowards?"

After the Confederate victory at the Battle of Chancellorsville in early May 1863, Milroy and his superiors in Washington and Harpers Ferry debated what to do about Winchester. Washington believed that Winchester should only be used as an outpost against enemy raids on the Baltimore and Ohio Railroad. Milroy wanted to use it as a launching pad for an invasion of the Upper Shenandoah Valley. While the two sides debated, Milroy completed the fortification of the town.

The Confederates were also debating what to do next. Vicksburg, Mississippi, was under siege, and the government in Richmond wanted to send troops to relieve the siege. General Robert E. Lee believed that a successful invasion of Pennsylvania would force the Union army to withdraw a substantial number of forces from Vicksburg to return east to protect the capital. Lee's plan won out, and General Richard Ewell and the Second Corps were ordered to clear the Shenandoah Valley in advance of the army's movement into Pennsylvania.

With the advance of the Second Corps, the men of the Stonewall Brigade were returning to their beloved Valley. Among these was Colonel John H.S. Funk, who had served as the commander of the brigade during the final days of the Battle of Chancellorsville, when General Elisha F. Paxton, the brigade's commander, was killed. As the brigade moved north toward Winchester, General James A. Walker replaced Funk as the permanent commander. Ironically, Walker, while a student at VMI, had challenged one of his instructors, Major Thomas J. Jackson, to a duel. Fortunately for both, the future "Stonewall" refused the challenge and had Walker expelled.

Arriving south of Winchester on June 13, Ewell employed a double envelopment against Milroy to secure the town. He sent General Jubal Early's division west and moved General "Allegheny" Johnson's division east of town, hoping to cut off Milroy's retreat. Both movements were successful, and by the end of June 14 Winchester's most hated occupation commander was utterly defeated in one of the most lopsided battles of the war.

Milroy and his staff managed to escape to Harpers Ferry, but his command lost nearly four thousand men, most of whom became prisoners. Milroy, who had made it his business to persecute the women and children of Winchester, abandoned his own noncombatants. Although Mrs. Milroy had left town several weeks before Ewell arrived, forty-seven wives and children of other Union officers at Winchester were left behind and captured by the Confederate army. Taken to Richmond, they were later exchanged at Annapolis, Maryland, and most felt that it was only a matter of time before the Federal government would collapse.

The Godfrey Miller House on Loudoun (Main) Street, the home of Gettie Miller and her sister, Emma, taken about thirty years after the war. Gettie is standing between the columns just to the right of the front door, and Emma is standing under the column just to the left of the door. *WFCHS.*

"Can It Be Possible that We Are a Nation of Cowards?"

It was during this period that Gettie Miller, a young girl who lived across the street from Kate Sperry and Tillie Russell, began to keep a diary. Just a child, she and her older sister, Emma, were playmates with Kate's younger sister, Jennie. The diary only covers five and a half months from May 1863 to mid-September 1863. Gettie's perspective of events, seen through the eyes of a child, was unique among the Winchester diarists, and it may give the best picture of what life was like for the citizens of Winchester during the war.

On the last day of May 1863, she recorded the death of a small child: "Aunt Lottie came here and said Nannie Bushnell was dead she said she died so hard they think the fever went to her brain. Nellie could not stop crying…I expect she will be so lonesome without Nannie to play with her." The very next day, she wrote that "Mrs. Gibson's little baby is dead. It was so little that they put it in little Sara's grave."

The first thing Gettie mentioned every day was the weather, because rain helped wash away the filth in the streets and cleaned the air of the smells of the sick and dying. On June 10, she observed that "the Yankees came around with a wagon and threw a pile of lime at nearly every house in this neighborhood." After the Second Battle of Winchester on June 13, she commented, "I do not want any of them killed I want them to go back to their homes and stay there." In August, Gettie witnessed the coldblooded murder of a civilian by Union soldiers: "They shot an old man in the road because he said to them (in fun) stop boys and give the rebbies a chance." She also added that the old man was drunk.

Her comments about her fellow townspeople were surprisingly honest. She was happy when her sister Emma

Kate Sperry's home on Loudoun (Main) Street. *GQ/BR.*

was invited to spend the night with Jennie Sperry—although it forced Jennie's big sister, Kate, to spend the night at Tillie Russell's house next door to make room—because it was "nice to have the bed all to myself." After going to church in mid-August, she complained because the preacher "is such a drone." She also reported that one of the wealthier women in town was wandering around downtown so drunk that she could barely stand and was chiding the people trying to help her because she owned slaves and they did not.

Gettie's main concern, however, was the breakdown of the school system in town. She wished that "the war would be over by school time" and was afraid, if it did not, that "we will grow up to be dumb." Her hopes were finally realized in mid-September when the diary abruptly ends. She had no time for it since the school at Grace Lutheran Church had reopened. She did, however, complain about her teacher, Mrs. Eichelberger, who placed Gettie and her sister Emma in seats on the opposite sides of the room from each other.

With the defeat of Milroy and the arrival of the Confederate army in June, Unionist despair was overwhelming. Lee's army seemed invincible, and the gloating of Southern sympathizers in town encouraged that belief. With Lee's army moving north into Pennsylvania, it looked like the war was going to end badly for the Unionists in Winchester.

Just five blocks up the street from Gettie Miller, Unionist Julia Chase's depression was growing with each day. Knowing that the Union army in Virginia had failed to defeat Lee's army in every engagement it had fought, she lamented on June 20: "Is the whole Federal army asleep or lain down their arms." On the Fourth of July, her heart broken, she reached out to God and wrote this prayer in her diary:

> *Our hope is all gone and we cannot expect but that a few days will determine the fate of Baltimore and Washington, that our Government is not able to maintain itself. Oh God! Thou art just, that our wickedness is so great, that our Country's cause cannot be a just and righteous one and that thou art arrayed against us. If thou be not for us, who shall stand? Have mercy, we beseech thee upon us. Gen Grant, it is said had also been defeated at Vicksburg. If our armies cannot succeed better, it would be far preferable that peace should follow than to sacrifice so many lives, and be considered a disgrace forever. How can we expect much from our soldiers when we fear that the Pennsylvanians instead of making a bold resistance to the invaders who are now in their State, instead of boldly defending their homes and firesides, ingloriously run away into other states? Can it be possible that we are a nation of cowards?*

"Can It Be Possible that We Are a Nation of Cowards?"

Dr. Enoch Hunt, surgeon of the Second Mississippi Infantry and the future husband of Kate Sperry. *WFCHS.*

As Chase penned these bitter words, events were taking place that changed the nature of the war. Lee's move into Pennsylvania was a desperate gamble and had failed miserably. After three days of the bloodiest fighting ever seen on the North American continent, his army was decisively defeated at Gettysburg. At the very moment that Chase wrote those melancholy words, Lee's army was beginning its retreat back to Virginia. On the same day, Grant accepted the surrender of the Confederate garrison at Vicksburg, placing the entire Mississippi River under Union control.

For Winchester, Lee's defeat meant another influx of wounded soldiers, and they began to arrive just three days after Chase's despondent diary entry. Fortunately for Kate Sperry, Dr. Enoch Hunt was not with the Second Mississippi Infantry at Gettysburg, having transferred to a hospital in Goldsboro, North Carolina, earlier in the year. His regiment had been badly mauled on the first day of the battle. Although she still had several beaus writing her on a regular basis, Hunt seemed to be the most persistent one.

For the Barton family, news from the battlefield was overshadowed by a tragedy at home. David Barton, the family patriarch, had been in ill health since the beginning of the war. Shortly after the Confederate army's return from Gettysburg, he finally died, leaving his wife with even more to grieve about. She had lost two sons, a brother and now her husband. Her grief and fears must have been crushing. With two sons, Randolph and Strother, still with the army, her only consolation was that Robert and her youngest son, Bolling, were out of harm's way. Bolling had been sent to VMI early in the war, as the family had refused to send all of their sons into the Confederate army.

General Lee and his army did not stay long in the Shenandoah Valley after Gettysburg. With it unlikely that the Union army would follow him there, he retreated to behind the Rapidan River less than three weeks after arriving at the Valley town. All of the wounded who could be moved were sent farther south to avoid their capture by the pursuing Union cavalry, and within just a few days of Lee's departure, the Union cavalry began to enter the town. Despite this quick occupation of Winchester, authorities in Washington had changed their position once again on the importance of the town.

The Federal government now saw little need to occupy Winchester with a Union garrison. To conciliation, harshness and vengeance was now added indifference. This new phase had dire consequences. Banks, Jackson and Milroy were now replaced by small Union cavalry detachments, Confederate guerrillas and partisan rangers, many of whom were nothing more than common thieves. The next nine months proved to be the most trying ones for the town, as opposing forces entered town on a daily basis, sometimes fighting in the streets and at other times harassing the citizens and robbing them or using them as pawns in a brutal game of retaliation.

For Cornelia McDonald, this proved to be too much. Trying to take care of a house full of children while fighting off competing bands of undisciplined cutthroats was something she could not face. Shortly after Lee's army left Winchester, she packed her children and what belongings she could carry and left for Lexington, Virginia. She was still melancholy about the decision to abandon her friends. On July 18, 1863, she wrote that they "drove down the avenue and turned into the road for the long, long journey. Heavy-hearted I was, for I knew nothing of what was before me, and I felt that I had let go the only hold I had on anything."

McDonald was not alone. Many people wanted no part of another Union occupation or guerrilla activity and were leaving as fast as they could. Ann C.R. Jones, Mrs. Barton's mother-in-law, commented that "so many persons are anxious to leave it, selling their houses and even old inhabitants, keen to go away." The small Union cavalry detachments that did enter Winchester during this period all observed that the town seemed deserted, with many dwellings empty, few people in the streets and even fewer businesses open.

"Can It Be Possible that We Are a Nation of Cowards?"

The Taylor Hotel, taken shortly after the war. *GQ/BR.*

Winchester, once a prosperous community that had fought to keep its little town in the Union while the country was declining into civil war, was now on the verge of collapse as so many of its citizens departed. Those who were leaving had good reason to go. As the Confederacy slowly and painfully died around them, suffering became a way of life. For the next twenty months, those who remained faced their fate with a stoic courage that has rarely been matched. It would transform the women, old men and children who lived there during this period from housekeepers, mothers, merchants and farmers into the stuff of legend. Simply put, their perseverance under these, the most difficult of circumstances, saved Winchester.

Kate McVicar described the next nine months as "the worst time of the war for the citizens of the county. What one side spared the other took. Those raiding parties, came so quietly that people had rarely any time to get things out of their way." Winchester changed hands almost daily; at least on one occasion it changed hands thirteen times in a single day. Confederate partisans fought the Union cavalry in the streets and in the countryside, and deserters and the scum of society took advantage of the total breakdown of law and order to ply their trades of robbery and murder unmolested.

Harriet Griffith, who had temporarily ceased keeping her diary in the spring of 1862, along with her family were the victims of one of these acts of brutality. Julia Chase recorded in her diary on January 18, 1864, that "rebels went to Mr. Griffith's house, broke his door open and threatened to blow his daughter's brains out." She continued: "Mr. Haines, a Union man, was robbed of $40, and his boots stolen by the same rascals. This is a dreadful way of living. We know not what an hour may bring forth."

It was not just the Unionists who were threatened, though. Joseph Sherrard, who lived on Loudoun Street in the center of downtown Winchester, was robbed of $200 in his own home. Mrs. Lee listened quietly in the middle of the night as soldiers cut down her fence for firewood. She rationalized that "[t]hey robbed the Union people too." Major Harry Gilmor, who was nominally in command of the Confederate partisans in the area, was powerless to control them. Although several suggestions were put forth, nothing seemed to work, and the criminal activity continued unabated.

When Confederate partisans broke into a house and arrested William Dooley, a suspected spy for Milroy, Union authorities finally decided to act. After Dooley's arrest, Union cavalry entered town and arrested several prominent citizens to hold as hostages for Dooley's return. Robert Y.

The Robert Y. Conrad Home on Market Street. *GQ/BR.*

"Can It Be Possible that We Are a Nation of Cowards?"

Conrad and Andrew Boyd were arrested. But before they could be sent to Martinsburg, Unionists in town, worried that this would simply lead to more violent acts against them by Confederate partisans, asked for their release. Boyd and Conrad were particularly singled out for house searches and arrests whenever the Union army needed hostages. This, however, was only the beginning of a series of arrests of Confederate sympathizers in town that did not end until the surrender at Appomattox.

The Union cavalry were not completely innocent of atrocities, though. Jacob Ritter, an elderly gentleman, was accosted by Union soldiers in late 1863. Chase stated that "three men dressed as soldiers came into town this morning, after robbing several persons on the Martinsburg Road of their money and horses and demanded the horse of Mr. Ritter." Ritter refused and ran for Legge's mill on Market Street. When George Legge tried to intercede, "they fired at him, wounding him in the arm and struck their sabers across his head." Chase continued: "Not satisfied with this, they went across the street to Mr. Sidwell's, breaking in the door and taking fire out, took it across to the mill and set it on fire." They then escaped, leaving Legge, who had lost one son at the Battle of Fredericksburg and another severely wounded at the Battle of Gaines' Mill, with his place of business in ruins.

If these daily occurrences were not bad enough, Winchester still had to deal with the continuous problem of disease and the never-ending loss of loved ones in battle. Less than four months after losing her husband, Mrs. Barton received the news that her son Strother had been badly wounded in the leg at the Battle of Mine Run. His leg had been amputated, and he was sent to Staunton, Virginia, to convalesce. Later that year, Strother's sister, Fanny, traveled to Staunton to visit relatives and care for her brother. On March 15, 1864, the twenty-four-year-old girl who was suffering from tuberculosis wrote a chatty letter to her brother Robert on her plans to travel with Strother to Lexington, Virginia: "My cough has been so much better for several days that Dr. Baldwin says there will be no objection to my offing if the weather is good."

After talking of money and Strother's care, she began to gossip about prospective beaus: "I like Cary's friend, Carter Berkely better than any of them when he is sober…John Opie is handsome but conceited and not smart." Her letter continued with a firm statement that, despite all of the attention she was receiving, her affection for one gentleman superseded all others and that she would remain loyal to him. The sad fact was that the journey to visit Strother had done nothing to abate the illness that was killing her, and Strother never truly recovered from his wound. Her chatty letters to Winchester, which she knew would be read by her mother, were probably meant to hide the reality of the situation and dispel her grief.

Despite all of the daily suffering from bandits, Confederate partisans and Union cavalrymen bent on retaliation, at least one Winchester resident found time for courting. Kate Sperry was still receiving a lot of attention from Dr. Hunt through the fall and winter of 1863–64, and the attention probably helped distract her from the terrifying events happening around her. In November 1863, she revealed in her diary that she "answered Dr. Hunt's letters as sweet as I knew how—I don't believe that I care one cent for him—He isn't my style. I don't love him—sometimes I think I do and again when I analyse my feelings I'm sadly puzzled to know whether I do or not—if I should never get another letter from him I don't believe I'd care one straw." The young doctor had obviously caught the Winchester coquette's attention.

Just a few days later, she wrote, "Never was more astonished in all my life than, upon opening a letter handed to me this morning, it should be from Dr. Hunt—nearly died (almost) over it." Four days later, she wrote in her diary, "Answered Dr. H's letter today—hadn't much to say—a dry old letter, but it's my only chance for peace and quietness for a week." Even though she insisted that she "[did] not love him" and didn't care "one straw" for his letters, she nevertheless sent lots of hints for him to continue. In her diary and in her letters to him, she insisted on telling him about all of the attention she was giving to soldiers from his native Mississippi during her daily visits to the hospital, and when one Mississippian, who happened to be very attractive, began receiving attention from several local girls, she immediately turned her attention to a soldier from North Carolina, where the good doctor was stationed.

For Kate Sperry and the rest of Winchester, spring was coming, and love would come with it—and not just for the beautiful young girl on Loudoun Street. It would also, however, bring the most momentous and earth-shattering events of the history of the little Valley town.

Chapter 8

"A Night on the Battlefield"

W hile Winchester was coping with the hardships of total war, and
Kate Sperry was attempting to decide what to do about the interest
shown her by a certain Mississippi doctor, events were transpiring elsewhere
that would again change conditions in the Shenandoah Valley. As spring
dawned, Winchester was about to experience the bloodiest period of its Civil
War existence, and fortunately, it also proved to be the last.

The first incident of the spring of 1864 was another arrest of Robert
Y. Conrad and Andrew Boyd, this time along with Philip Williams, the
law partner of the late David Barton. Taken to Martinsburg, they were
allowed to stay with friends until an arrest by Confederate partisans of
three Unionists in nearby Morgan County escalated the situation. In
retaliation, Conrad and his two companions were sent to the state prison
in Wheeling, West Virginia. Conrad was allowed to go to Richmond and
seek an exchange for the three Morgan County captives in return for his
and his two friends' release.

It must have been difficult for Julia Chase to have much sympathy for
her pastor, Reverend Boyd. In January, she had received the shocking news
of her father's sudden death. He had just left for a trip west when the news
came. She lamented in her diary: "Oh, to think that we were not permitted
to see his face again, or hear his last dying words. We feel the rebels have
been the cause of his death, never having been the same person since he
was taken prisoner by them." She dryly commented in her diary on April 24
that "Dr. Boyd and Mr. Williams are in prison at Wheeling, receiving prison

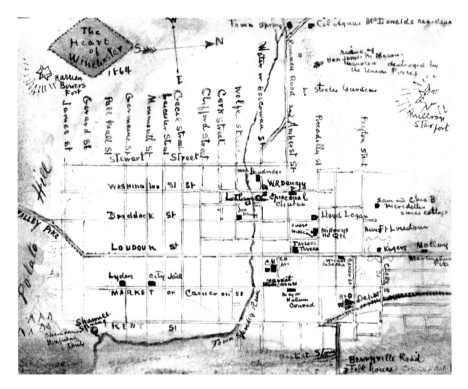

A Winchester map drawn by a Union soldier in 1864. *THL.*

fare, have not been sent to Ohio as we heard." Unlike prior arrests, their stay there turned out to be a long one.

After his victories at Vicksburg and Chattanooga in the Western Theater, President Lincoln sent for General Ulysses S. Grant, hoping that he could duplicate his success in Virginia against General Robert E. Lee. The strategy that Grant employed was not new. Union generals had unsuccessfully tried to defeat Lee and capture Richmond since 1861. What was different in 1864 was that Lee's army had almost been bled white from three years of fighting, and Grant was more determined than any general before him to destroy Lee and capture Richmond. Grant intended to make war not just on Lee's army but on everything that sustained it, too.

Grant's plan included three offensive movements designed to overwhelm the Confederates with numbers and destroy their ability to fight. One army, under General Benjamin Butler, moved from Fort Monroe on the Atlantic directly to the Virginia capital. Grant, with the Army of the Potomac, attacked Lee in central Virginia. The third movement, by General Franz

Sigel, was another invasion of the Shenandoah Valley to destroy the crops and livestock that were feeding Lee's army. Grant's plan, however, began to unravel almost immediately. Butler failed to take Richmond and was easily bottled up just southeast of the capital. After nearly three weeks of some of the bloodiest fighting of the war, Grant was stymied near Spotsylvania County Courthouse. But like all of the other battles fought in Virginia over the last three years, even victories were accompanied by sorrow for Winchester.

On May 12, 1864, a massive attack by the Union army at Spotsylvania had resulted in disaster for the Stonewall Brigade. Trapped in what was known as the "Muleshoe Salient," most of the brigade was either slaughtered or captured, including its division commander, General "Allegheny" Johnson. After the fighting, the Stonewall Brigade was totally devoid of field grade officers, and many Winchester soldiers were among those captured. In the Fifth Virginia Infantry, Lieutenant William "Billy" Funk, the brother of Colonel John H.S. Funk, was among them, as was Captain G.W. Kurtz. Charles E. Bell of the Second Virginia Infantry (the next-door neighbor of Robert Y. Conrad) and Edward J. Reed of Chew's Battery (the son of the mayor of Winchester) were among those taken prisoner. Colonel Funk, fortunately, was not captured.

The very week of the disaster at Spotsylvania, one of Mrs. Barton's sons, Bolling, experienced his first battle. Sent to VMI to spare at least one of their sons, he was caught up in General Franz Sigel's invasion of the Valley at the Battle of New Market. Called up for duty during the emergency, Bolling joined his fellow cadets in their celebrated charge on May 15 that broke Sigel's line and forced him to make a quick retreat. Although Bolling was not injured, the charge cost the cadet corps ten killed and forty-seven wounded. Among the dead was Thomas G. Jefferson, the grandson of Thomas Jefferson.

Relief over the safety of Bolling was short-lived. His sister, Fanny, was suffering badly from tuberculosis at her grandmother's home, Vaucluse. Robert Barton recorded in his memoirs: "My sister had had a dreadful hemorrhage and was very weak; but I can see her bright and cheerful face as she fondly greeted me. She was all happiness, and never have I seen or heard of any body who seemed to be going so delightedly." The reason for her happiness was her belief that what was happening to her was "to be a most glorious consummation of all the hopes her religion held out for her."

Fanny died on May 29 and was buried at Vaucluse. Her next-door neighbor, Mrs. Lee, wrote, "How I envy her heavenly rest, I can imagine her united with her father, sister, and her brothers." Later that summer, Major

Vaucluse, the home of Ann Cary Randolph Jones and the burial site of Fanny Barton. *GQ/BR.*

Thomas Marshall, who was married to Fanny's sister until her death shortly before the war, wrote in his condolences to Robert Barton that his moments with Fanny were "most precious and shall ever be preserved as such." He spoke of her "joy of the Lord" and lamented that "[n]o more for us does the bright eye sparkle, or do we hear the tones of the much-loved or feel the pressure of her gentle hand." Fanny's letter to Robert in late 1863, referring to her loyalty to her true love, probably concerned Major Marshall. The Barton family, however, disapproved since Marshall was the widower of Fanny's sister.

While Winchester was grieving for the death or capture of its loved ones, on May 24 General David Hunter passed through Winchester on his way to relieve Sigel. His arrival marked a decided change for the worse for the people of the Valley. Grant was determined to eliminate the Shenandoah Valley as a source of supplies for the Confederate army, and Hunter was equally determined to do it. Under his command, the Union army began a systematic burning of everything considered useful to the Confederate army. Burning mills and crops and slaughtering livestock along the way, he defeated a small Confederate force under General William "Grumble" Jones at the Battle of Piedmont on June 5. With nothing to stop him, Hunter continued his path of destruction to Lexington, where Cornelia McDonald and her husband, Angus, were living, burning VMI and the home of Virginia governor John Letcher while there. Cornelia was forced to flee. Her husband, however, was captured. His imprisonment proved to be too much for the sixty-four-year-old, and he died shortly after being exchanged that year.

After sacking Lexington, Hunter moved east toward Lynchburg, where he intended to destroy railroads, canals and Confederate hospitals. Instead, he met General Jubal Early and the Second Corps of the Army of Northern Virginia. Succeeding General Richard Ewell, who was ill, Early commanded the corps for the remainder of 1864, through the bloodiest fighting the Shenandoah Valley had ever seen. He decisively defeated Hunter on June 19 and forced him to flee into West Virginia. With his path now clear, Early and the Second Corps could head north toward Winchester and beyond.

General Jubal Early commanded Confederate forces in the Shenandoah Valley during the summer and fall of 1864. *GQ/BR.*

A superb combat officer, Early had risen quickly in the Confederate army, commanding a division in the Second Corps until briefly assigned to command the Third Corps of Lee's army after the Battle of the Wilderness, when General A.P. Hill was too sick to continue. Promoted to lieutenant general and in command of the Second Corps, Early wasted little time moving north. His objective was similar to Stonewall Jackson's two years before: to cause such a stir that President Lincoln would fear for the safety of Washington.

Entering Winchester on July 2, Early's men purposely passed by Mrs. Lee's home as a sign of respect. Leaving the very next day, he took his army into Maryland and on July 9 defeated a Union force under General Lew Wallace at the Battle of Monocacy, just east of Frederick, Maryland. Early eventually took his army to the outskirts of Washington but was unable to capture the city. Making a quick retreat through Leesburg, Virginia, he was back in the Shenandoah Valley by mid-July. His brief campaign was an amazing feat, but it had dire consequences.

Reinforced by the Sixth Corps from the trenches at Petersburg, the Union forces pursuing Early under the command of General George Crook fought a nasty rear guard action at Cool Spring on July 18 near the Shenandoah River in Clarke County. Then disaster struck. Retreating to Winchester, General Stephen Ramseur, commanding one of Early's divisions, was badly beaten at the Battle of Rutherford Farm just north of Winchester. His defeat forced the evacuation of Winchester by Early's army.

For Winchester, the two battles inundated the town with casualties. After Early's raid on Washington, the Union commander at Rutherford Farm was in no mood to show mercy. Refusing to allow the Confederates to remove their dead and wounded from the battlefield at Rutherford Farm, it fell to the women of Winchester to provide any care they could. When Confederate surgeons entered Winchester seeking help, Kate Sperry's next-door neighbor Tillie Russell volunteered. It was a decision that transformed her from just another young lady in town to a Winchester legend.

There are numerous accounts of Russell's actions on the Rutherford Farm battlefield, and almost none agree on what really happened. Many of the accounts are obviously fiction. One even records her death shortly after the battle. What remains, however, is truly amazing. Tillie's sister, Lucy, probably gave the most credible account, and it is used here.

Shortly after the battle, Dr. Love came into Winchester seeking volunteers to go to the battlefield and care for the more than sixty wounded Confederates. Russell, along with twenty other women, volunteered and walked four miles

Tillie Russell, taken several years after the war. *GQ/BR.*

to the battlefield. Noticing that an officer, named Randolph Ridgely, was badly wounded by a bullet that had broken his hip, Love asked Russell to care for him until he returned. He told her to cradle his head in her lap and that if he had any chance to live she had to "[k]eep him quiet. Don't let him move. He ought to stay perfectly still all night." He also told her that this was his only chance for survival.

The doctor failed to tell Tillie when he would return, and she remained with Ridgely the entire night, staying perfectly still while the young officer slept in her lap. At dawn, Love returned and, amazed at Russell's perseverance, marveled, "My Lord, child. You been up all night." When she replied, "Yes, sir," he said, "Well, I believe you have saved his life. He's better." Putting the exhausted Russell and the wounded Ridgely in his carriage, he brought them back to Winchester. The experience left Russell bedridden for several days, but she recovered and lived until the end of the century.

Russell's heroic act went unnoticed for many years. Kate Sperry, although she mentioned Tillie frequently in her diary, never commented about this incident. It was, after all, what all of the women in Winchester had been doing since March 1862. Several years after the war, an artist and

A Night on the Battlefield depicts Tillie Russell caring for Lieutenant Randolph Ridgeley after the Battle of Rutherford Farm, July 20, 1864. *WFCHS.*

Confederate veteran named Oregon Wilson made a sketch of Russell's act that he titled *A Night on the Battlefield.* When several Confederate veterans from the Valley, such as John Esten Cooke, wrote about it, Russell's fame spread far and wide, and today she is known among Winchester residents as the "Angel of the Battlefield."

Sperry can be forgiven for not noticing Russell's "night on the battlefield." Her mind was cluttered during the entire year from a shocking letter she received from North Carolina. On February 27, she recorded in her diary, "I got a letter from Dr. Hunt, <u>in which he asks me to marry him, after the war</u>—says we've been corresponding sometime and it's nothing more than proper to ask for a further understanding." She continued, saying that she was "surprised to receive it—don't know what to say—would rather he had not written it, for I'm most afraid to say <u>yes</u> and don't want to say <u>no</u>. I've got the blues most miserably from it." That night, she added to her diary, "Wrote to Jo and answered Theodore's letter—and now that other one is <u>to be did</u>—it certainly will be the 'hardest work of my life.'"

For a young lady whose diary is nearly perfect in its diction, for her to write "to be did" confirms her confusion. True to her word, the next day she wrote, "Answered Dr. Hunt's letter and told him <u>YES</u> without any ado, but I'm certain I didn't write it as sensible as he—hope he'll get it—so now <u>I've sent and gone and done it</u>!" On May 5, Sperry received a letter from Hunt that let her know in no uncertain terms that he "got it": "[Y]ou cannot conceive how much pleasure and happiness it affords me to know that I can with confidence call you 'my own.' My pride is flattered. My soul is full of real pleasure and I feel in every way a happier and better man."

While Tillie Russell was making history and Kate Sperry was adapting to her new role as fiancée to a Mississippi doctor, General Jubal Early was plotting to reverse his army's defeat at Rutherford Farm. On July 24, using a double envelopment similar the one that Ewell had employed a year before at the Second Battle of Winchester, Early crushed Crook's Union army on the old Kernstown battlefield, forcing him to retreat across the Potomac River into Maryland. Early followed his victory at Kernstown by ordering cavalry commander General John McCausland to enter Pennsylvania to seek revenge for Hunter's arson earlier in the year. On July 30, Chambersburg went up in flames thanks to McCausland's handiwork, and the stakes got even higher in the Shenandoah Valley.

Early's victory confounded General Ulysses S. Grant, whose army was bogged down in a stalemate with General Robert E. Lee's army in front of Petersburg. It seemed that every Union general from Banks to Crook could not defeat the stubborn Confederate soldiers from the Shenandoah Valley, and its resources still flowed to the Confederate army. Grant had brought General Philip Sheridan with him from the west to command the cavalry of the Army of the Potomac. Like the Union army in the Valley, the cavalry of the Army of the Potomac was no match for its Confederate counterpart under General J.E.B. Stuart.

Sheridan, when finally given a chance after the Battle of the Wilderness, proved that he was more than a match for Stuart. On May 11, 1864, he not only defeated the Confederate cavalry at the Battle of Yellow Tavern, just north of Richmond, but also killed his greatest adversary, Stuart. After the battle, Grant gave Sheridan the task of clearing the Shenandoah Valley, ordering him to destroy it completely as a source of supplies to the Confederacy.

At the head of an army of forty thousand men, Sheridan took command in the Shenandoah Valley on August 6. He had risen through the ranks during the war from a staff officer to the rank of major general and commander of an army. His performance in combat, from Murfreesboro to Missionary Ridge, made his reputation as a fighting general second to none.

The stakes, however, were never higher, and he showed great caution. As August turned into September, the 1864 presidential election was just two months away, and war weariness was profound in the North. If Lincoln

General Philip Sheridan commanded the Union army in the Shenandoah Valley during the summer and fall of 1864. *GQ/BR.*

lost the election, his opponent, George B. McClellan, promised to negotiate peace with the South. A defeat at the hands of the Confederates would almost ensure McClellan's election. With victory or defeat in the balance, and both the North and the South pinning their hopes on the coming battle in the Shenandoah Valley, a young Quaker girl from Winchester was about to make history.

Chapter 9

"No Better Dust Lies in Mount Hebron Cemetery"

Rebecca Wright was not the type of person one would expect to be the purveyor of great events like battles or presidential elections. She lived quietly on Loudoun Street, and like all of the young ladies of Winchester, she went daily to the hospitals around town to care for the sick and wounded. A Quaker, like her friend Harriet Griffith, she was passionately opposed to war in all forms and abhorred the institution of slavery. A loyal Unionist throughout the war, she suffered the same indignities that the others in town had suffered at the hands of those who supported the Confederacy.

She, like Harriet and probably everyone else in Winchester, was sick of the fighting and dying. Griffith, who began her diary again shortly after Sheridan took command near Winchester, was still caring for the wounded Union soldiers in town. One in particular attracted her attention: a desperately wounded young soldier named Lea. On August 23, she recorded: "Went to the hospital as usual. Lea had such a dreadful chill. He kept me by him all the time and did not want me to leave." The next day she "[t]ook Lea a big breakfast and saw all of the men as usual."

To her surprise, a few days later, she wrote, "Went to see the Lt. and take him breakfast, and then to see poor Lea. He could hardly talk. I gave him some tea and he said he knew me and called me by my name, Harriet Griffith, and said it was a pretty name." She went on: "Stayed there as long as I could. It made me feel so sad and badly and I would think and think about poor Lea." Later that day, she returned to the hospital: "Had supper, then Mary Jane and I went around to the hospital and found Lea dead. He

Rebecca Wright, a Quaker girl who passed information on to General Sheridan, bringing about the Third Battle of Winchester. *THL.*

had died at two o'clock. He did not say anything after I left. Poor fellow. It did make me feel so badly, for I knew him so well and he thought so much of me, too." As Harriet was about to leave, several of the Union wounded in the room asked her "to write his wife soon."

With shared experiences like this occurring on a regular basis, it is little wonder that Harriet's friend, whom she called Becky, decided to act. General Early's Confederate army was well positioned around Winchester, and his force was augmented by General Joseph Kershaw's division from the Army of Northern Virginia. Sheridan waited patiently outside town for an opening to attack. With Sheridan inactive, General Robert E. Lee, with his forces around Petersburg stretched to near breaking, ordered Kershaw and his division to return. It was a desperate gamble, leaving Early with just twelve thousand men to face Sheridan's forty thousand, but Lee believed that it was necessary.

On September 16, a free African American named Tom Laws slipped Wright a note from Sheridan, asking for information on troops' dispositions: "Have any troops arrived from Richmond, or are any more coming, or reported to be coming." The note made Wright extremely nervous, but with so much at stake, she decided to act. Having heard, from convalescing Confederate soldiers, that Anderson's division had left that very day for Richmond, when Laws returned the next day, she sent the reply: "General Anderson's commanding, have been sent away, and no more are expected, as they cannot be spared from Richmond." Despite referring to Kershaw's division as belonging to Anderson, the note astounded Sheridan, who could not believe his good fortune. It was the intelligence he was waiting for, and he immediately ordered an attack on Winchester with his entire army for the morning of September 19.

Despite outnumbering his Confederate opponent by more than two to one, Sheridan faced a daunting challenge. Before him was the Second Corps of the Army of Northern Virginia, which Stonewall Jackson had molded into one of the most feared military organizations ever to fight on the North American continent. Within that corps was the remnant of the old Stonewall Brigade. Although reduced in numbers due to its heavy fighting and its near extermination at Spotsylvania, it was still full of fight and was defending the very Valley town that "Stonewall" loved the most, next to his hometown of Lexington.

For this battle, the brigade, along with fourteen other regiments, was consolidated within General William Terry's brigade, which was also heavily reduced in numbers. The contingent making up what once was the Stonewall Brigade was under the command of Winchester native Colonel John H.S. Funk. The division was commanded by General John B. Gordon, a seasoned fighter whose wife was staying at Mrs. Lee's home in downtown Winchester.

There were also many soldiers in Early's command who were determined to give their best effort because the women of Winchester had cared for them and brought them back to health from sickness or battlefield wounds. What Sheridan faced at dawn on September 19, 1864, were twelve thousand of the best soldiers ever to grace a battlefield, defending a town they loved with all of their heart. One way or the other, it was going to be a bloody day.

Sheridan had one advantage that failed to materialize. Early had sent a large segment of his command to Martinsburg, and if he could break the Confederate line before their return, it would be an easy victory. Forced to travel through a narrow passageway known as Berryville Canyon to get to Winchester from the east, Sheridan was delayed, allowing Early to assemble all of his forces before Sheridan could attack. Sheridan began the battle with an attack along the Berryville Pike, with General Horatio Wright's

Colonel John Henry Funk, a Winchester doctor who commanded the Fifth Virginia Infantry, Stonewall Brigade. *GQ/BR.*

Veterans of the Marion Rifles, Company A, Fifth Virginia Infantry, Stonewall Brigade, taken in 1894 in front of the Frederick County Courthouse. This company was originally commanded by Colonel John H.S. Funk. *WFCHS.*

Sixth Corps. His plan was to slowly extend his attacks northward until the Confederate line was stretched too thin and broke.

The plan quickly miscarried, however, due to a wide gap between Wright's Sixth Corps and the Nineteenth Corps to the north. Seeing the mistake, the Confederates under Generals Gordon and Robert Rodes launched a vicious counterattack. Despite the clever move by the Confederates, overwhelming numbers forced them back. When another Union attack was launched even farther north later in the day, Gordon was forced to send his division back into the line of fire. The fighting around the Hackwood house, where Gordon sent his division, was desperate. Heavily outnumbered, Terry's brigade held on as long as it could.

When General Terry was wounded and forced to leave the field, Funk took command of the entire brigade. As the casualties began to mount, Funk exposed himself recklessly in an attempt to keep his command together and repel the assault on his hometown. While grappling with the enemy near Hackwood, the Winchester colonel was badly wounded. With the loss of both Terry and Funk, and the overwhelming forces being employed against them, Gordon and his division were forced to retreat to the inner defenses of Winchester. A massive cavalry charge on the Confederate left crushed its line, sending Early's entire army fleeing through the streets of Winchester.

From in front of Mrs. Lee's home, General Gordon's wife attempted to rally the retreating forces, but it was to no avail. Sheridan had pounded the Southern army relentlessly the entire day, and his larger numbers proved to be too much, even for the famed Second Corps. The horrific battle had taken a shocking toll. Two Confederate generals, Rodes and Archibald Godwin, had been killed, four others had been seriously wounded and nearly four thousand Confederate soldiers, representing one-third of Early's army, lay dead or wounded on the battlefield.

Casualties in the Union army were even more severe. General David Russell was killed in the fighting, and three other generals were seriously wounded. It cost Sheridan's army more than five thousand men to capture Winchester, as the Confederate army fought with desperation rarely seen in the Shenandoah Valley. Even after the Battle of Gettysburg, Winchester had not been faced with caring for more wounded, and the Gettysburg wounded were moved as quickly as possible to locations south of the town. This battle, however, was just the beginning. Later in the month, the two armies grappled again just south of Strasburg at Fisher's Hill, resulting in another Confederate defeat. Early retreated south to Rude's Hill, just north of New Market, to lick his wounds and prepare for whatever lay ahead.

The grave of Colonel John H.S. Funk in Mount Hebron Cemetery, Winchester, Virginia. *Photo by Ben Ritter.*

Taken to his parents' house on Market Street, Colonel Funk lingered for a couple of days before dying of his wound on September 21. He was twenty-four years old. To have a native son in command of the brigade that Stonewall Jackson had trained and commanded was no small honor, and the death of the popular colonel devastated Winchester. Through a tribute in a local newspaper signed by "M.E.," the townspeople poured out their hearts:

> *Few have fallen more beloved and lamented by his comrades than Col. Funk. He was a dutiful son, a devoted brother and a kind friend, and is now in that bright home where the clash of arms is never heard. And most sincerely does the writer of this notice pray that the God who sustains him in his last moments may pour the oil of His grace on the troubled waters of the hearts of his bereaved friends.*

Elisha Hunt Rhodes, a Union officer with the Second Rhode Island Infantry, while wandering through Mount Hebron Cemetery in Winchester, happened upon Colonel Funk's funeral. He recorded his reaction in his memoirs, *All for the Union*:

"No Better Dust Lies in Mount Hebron Cemetery"

I have taken a walk through the cemetery near the city, and my heart was sad as I passed the newmade graves of Confederate soldiers and saw the wreath of flowers which mourning hands placed there. As we walked around some trees we came upon a party of ladies and paroled Rebel officers. It was too late for us to retreat and so we removed our hats and stood near the party. The scene was a sad one, and the people looked at us as if we were intruding, but I did not feel that it would be right to leave and so remained. The dead man was Colonel Funk of Winchester.

Funk, whose father was a bricklayer and lived in a modest home several blocks south of the more illustrious Conrads, Bartons and Lees, had chosen to become a doctor, a man of healing. Studying at the Winchester Medical College, the young man whom his friends called "Stover" had graduated just one year before the war began and hardly had any time to practice his trade. Kate McVicar, years later, penned these few short words about her fallen friend: "No better dust lies in Mount Hebron Cemetery than that which was Col. Funk."

Unfortunately for the Funk family, their grief had just begun. "Billy" Funk, at about the same time as his brother's death, was suffering, if possible, even more. Far away in Charleston, South Carolina, a drama was unfolding that turned young Billy into a cruel pawn of war. After the Confederate army defending Charleston used fifty Union officers as human shields to protect the civilians in town from bombardment, the Union army besieging the city retaliated by bringing six hundred Confederate prisoners to Charleston to act as human shields on Morris Island. They hoped that this would silence the Confederate artillery at Fort Sumter.

Among the prisoners sent to Charleston was Lieutenant Jefferson William "Billy" Funk. There he remained for two months, living in an outdoor stockade under the fire of Confederate guns from Charleston. To make matters worse, the Confederate prisoners were put on a starvation diet in retaliation for the treatment of Union prisoners at Andersonville. With food scarce and sanitation even worse, it is little wonder that more Confederate prisoners died of starvation and disease during the two months than from Confederate shells.

In late October, Funk and his fellow prisoners were shipped to Fort Pulaski for another two months. Thirteen died of dysentery and scurvy while there. Captain J. Ogden Murray of the Eleventh Virginia Cavalry and a fellow prisoner described Funk as "little more than a boy. A Gallant brave boy, he was captured at the Battle of Spotsylvania, reaching Fort Delaware just in time to be selected as one of the six hundred." He continued: "The rigors of retaliation worked very hard, and soon completely broke him down."

Lieutenant Jefferson William "Billy" Funk, one of the "Immortal 600." *GQ/BR.*

Funk survived the ordeal at Fort Pulaski and was transferred back to Fort Delaware in March 1865, but the damage was done. Ogden said, "In his suffering with dysentery and scurvy Funk lost heart and nerve, slowly starving to death." He died on May 26, 1865, over a month after Lee's surrender at Appomattox and just two days after a visit from his mother. He and his fellow prisoners are remembered today as the "Immortal 600."

One Winchester resident who missed the battle and the subsequent occupation by Sheridan and his army was Kate Sperry. Since spring, the young lady had a lot on her mind. Her diary is filled with references to handsome young men and visits to friends, but it hardly represents reality. Her father was away most of the time serving as a sutler in the Confederate army, and she and her sister Jennie lived with her grandfather, Peter Sperry, who was nearing seventy years of age in 1864.

She began the war, like most of the young girls in town, enjoying the attention of the new recruits to the Confederate army who passed through or were stationed in Winchester. As the war progressed and many of those same young beaus were entering the cemetery at an alarming rate, she was forced to grow up quickly. Wrestling with the daily work at the hospitals and helping her grandfather take care of her younger sister, she obviously used her diary as a form of escape. While trying to decide what to do about her new romance with Dr. Enoch Hunt, she also was caring for an aging and sick grandfather who had been bedridden for nearly a year. On August 10, she wrote, "Grandpa had been very ill—Pa had to leave—and with only one servant and she half-way moron and Aunt Wardy not too well, Jen and I have had our hands full."

On August 13, she wrote, "Grandpa very ill—his sufferings have been great—poor old man—nearly one year in bed." The next day, "Grandpa died at 12 o'clock this morning—was more than willing to go—never saw any one more resigned—how deathlike he is—how we will miss him!" After the funeral the next day, she was "too sick at heart to write." Without an adult in the house, life became very difficult for Kate, even though her grandfather had been unable to be of much help.

On September 3, Aunt Scotia and George Deems arrived at the Sperry home with a letter from Dr. Hunt. Kate recorded in her diary on that same day that "Aunt Scotia wants me to go home with them to Goldsboro and I think it is my duty to go and see if I love 'Ed' as much as I think I do." On September 17, just two days before the battle that would wrench Winchester from Confederate hands forever and cost the life of Colonel Funk, she and her little sister Jennie took the stage to New Market after a "splendid serenade last night—kind of a farewell 'musicale.'"

While Sperry journeyed south, what was left of the once proud Second Corps of the Army of Northern Virginia was forced to watch helplessly as Sheridan and his army wreaked havoc on the Shenandoah Valley between Winchester and New Market. His systematic burning of everything useful to Confederate resistance was much more methodical and thorough than anything Hunter had done. When the Confederates finally recovered enough to make one more attempt at throwing Sheridan out of the Valley, they were forced to march to Winchester through an area that was as barren as a moon landscape.

Arriving at Fisher's Hill in mid-October, Early and his generals devised a bold plan to catch Sheridan's army by surprise and, hopefully, force it to retreat back across the Potomac River. The presidential election was just a couple of weeks away, and a stunning Confederate victory in the Shenandoah Valley might still turn the election against Lincoln. Still badly outnumbered, and his men having marched nearly forty miles without food, it was a gamble that had to be taken.

On October, 19, the Confederates launched their surprise attack against the vulnerable Union left flank near Cedar Creek. For several hours they drove the Union army north in disorder. To make the situation even more promising, Sheridan had just returned to Winchester from a meeting with Grant and was several miles away from the battlefield. While the Sixth Corps made a heroic stand at the Middletown Cemetery, just west of Middletown, Sheridan leaped on his horse and sped to the battlefield.

Sheridan's ride to the Cedar Creek battlefield became the stuff of legend and was the subject of a famous poem written after the war by Thomas Buchanan Reed. The reality was that after their initial success, the Confederates became bogged down by their own exhaustion and starvation. Stopping to grab food at abandoned Union camps, Early's army lost its momentum, and by the time Sheridan arrived, it was vulnerable to a counterattack. Late in the afternoon, with the commanding general now on the field, the Union army made that counterattack, throwing the Confederate army back across Cedar Creek and beyond in wild confusion.

The Battle of Cedar Creek was over, Lincoln's reelection was ensured and the Confederate hold on the Shenandoah Valley was over. Winchester had changed hands for the last time. For the Confederates in town, who still remained the majority, it was a devastating blow. For the Unionist minority, it was the answer to their prayers. There was still one enormous problem, though. The battles at Winchester and Cedar Creek filled Winchester with more wounded soldiers than ever before during the war. After the fighting began around Winchester on September 19, a continuous caravan of wounded soldiers from both armies filled the streets, homes and public buildings, and this continued until a few days after the Battle of Cedar Creek a month later.

In addition to public buildings such as churches and business establishments like the Taylor and Union Hotels, almost every private residence in the area was converted into a hospital. Kate McVicar's family, whose home was located near the final cavalry charge of the September 19 battle, was allowed only two rooms in their home. The rest were used for wounded soldiers. Mrs. Lee estimated that there were at least twenty new hospitals in use. Many of the soldiers were left on the battlefield due to a lack of facilities or transportation. Despite being ordered not to, many Winchester women ventured onto the battlefield on the evening after the battle to offer what help they could.

The bloody Battle of Cedar Creek a month later only compounded the problem. In the face of the continued presence of Confederate guerrillas in the area, Sheridan ordered the rebuilding of the Winchester and Potomac Railroad to help alleviate the shortages of supplies and medicines. This also allowed some of the wounded to be moved elsewhere. Only after the

The grave of Captain Hugh H. McGuire, Company E, Eleventh Virginia Cavalry. *Photo by Ben Ritter.*

beginning of 1865, three months after the battle at Winchester, did the situation finally come under control.

It took longer for Sheridan to stop the guerrilla activity. Colonel John S. Mosby had been operating in the Upper Shenandoah Valley since his arrival, and after Early's defeat he represented the only Confederate presence there. Sheridan tried almost every tactic he could think of to capture the elusive Rebel but failed miserably. Only Lee's surrender at Appomattox put an end to Mosby's raids on Union supplies.

Robert Y. Conrad, Philip Williams and Andrew Boyd returned from their incarceration at the Wheeling penitentiary at about the same time that the final battles in the Valley were being fought. Boyd was a broken man from the experience, both physically and psychologically. Julia Chase's pastor and frequent visitor to her home before the war only survived for a little less than a year, dying on December 16, 1865. Conrad continued to be a lightning rod for Union authorities and was arrested several times during the last months of the war.

For Harriet Griffith and her fellow Unionists in town, it was a season of celebration. Union officers from Sheridan on down threw parties on a regular basis and invited as many of the local girls as would come. Several enterprising Union officers even held parties with an invitation list that only included young ladies of the Confederate persuasion. Mrs. Lee, who stayed loyal to the South to the bitter end, was horrified when one of the young Confederate girls in town agreed to marry a Union officer.

Harriet, whose home was just a few houses down from General Sheridan's headquarters, received an enormous amount of attention from Union officers. The sleigh rides, parties and other amusements she invariably shared with Captain William Ellis of Sheridan's staff posed a serious problem for the Quaker girl when the two fell in love. Ellis was an Episcopalian, and Quakers were forbidden to marry outside the church. Love, however, triumphed over denominationalism, and the two were married on October 10, 1865.

For the Confederate supporters still in town, things were not quite as pleasant. With Mosby still on the prowl, anyone suspected of harboring his men was treated harshly. Sheridan went to the extreme measure of ordering all males under fifty be removed to behind Confederate lines in an attempt to put a stop to the activity. A number of Winchester residents were arrested and incarcerated at Fort McHenry in Maryland or dumped outside of town.

For Mrs. Lee, the end came in February 1865. Having grown weary of her constant activities in support of the Confederacy, Sheridan ordered her and her family removed from Winchester. Mrs. Lee, of course, described the event in great detail in her diary: "We laughed and talked all sorts of rebel talk and the Yankees gazed in astonishment at seeing people turned out of their homes and not depressed about it." When the procession entered Loudoun Street, "The whole street was filled with lookers-on: citizens, Yankees, servants—altogether a most motley assemblage."

As the spring campaign season began, Sheridan returned to command the Union cavalry in Grant's army outside Petersburg. His replacement was General Winfield Scott Hancock, one of the most distinguished officers of the war. When he was given word of Lee's surrender, Hancock ordered the town to be illuminated. A defiant Robert Y. Conrad stormed into his office upon hearing his order and stated, "Well, General Hancock, you can destroy every member of my family, and burn my house to the ground, but illuminate I will not."

Chapter 10

"The Stonewall Brigade"

A lthough the war years were a trying experience for Winchester, the years following the war were not nearly as bad for the Valley town as they were for the rest of the South. The secret to Winchester's success after the war is found in its activities prior to it. Although closely aligned with the South culturally, Winchester, since its earliest settlement in the mid-1700s, was economically tied to the North. With Sheridan's rebuilding of the Winchester and Potomac Railroad in 1864, the town was able to open the rich produce of the Valley again to northern markets like Baltimore and Philadelphia.

For these cities, as well as others, it was in their economic interest to help restore the town's prosperity as quickly as possible, and money and supplies poured into Winchester almost as soon as the fighting stopped at Appomattox. As time passed, the renewing of trade helped Winchester and Frederick County become some of the largest producers of wheat and produce in the world. The town also developed a strong woolen industry, which added to the town's prosperity and created needed jobs for its citizens.

One pressing necessity immediately after the war was to create a proper burial ground for the soldiers of both sides who had died in Winchester. Many were interred in unmarked graves near the battlefields around and in the town. Others were buried in people's backyards and near the various hospitals. The federal government immediately began work on a National Cemetery, and it was completed in 1866. After Gettysburg, it was the first of its kind in the United States.

National Cemetery, Winchester, Virginia; dedicated in 1866, it was the second of its kind after the Gettysburg National Cemetery. *WFCHS.*

Very soon after the war, a committee of prominent citizens was appointed to create a Confederate cemetery. Money was raised, land was acquired near the Mount Hebron Cemetery, coffins were built and arrangements were made for the removal of bodies. June 6, 1866, the fourth anniversary of General Turner Ashby's death, was set as the date for the first memorial service and included a funeral service and the reburial of Ashby at the new Winchester cemetery. His body was moved from Charlottesville, Virginia, where he was buried shortly after his death.

The ceremony on June 6, 1866, was the largest of its kind in the history of Winchester. Kate McVicar described the occasion:

> *The procession formed at the Episcopal Church at 11 a.m. Prayer was made by Norval Wilson. Colonel Richard, Capt. George W. Kurtz, James Burgess, Randolph Barton, J.C. Moore, Edward Trenary, E. Holmes Boyd, J.A. Nufton, Miller Wolfe, Stewart Steele, and J.I.H. Baker led the Winchester Brass Band, which had been recently organized. Fourteen young ladies, dressed in white, marched first, carrying wreaths. They had each lost a relative in battle. Remnants of the Stonewall Brigade, Ashby's Cavalry,*

"The Stonewall Brigade"

and Chew's Battery, numbering about 300 men, formed the escort. They were under the command of Col. L.T. Moore.

Also in the procession, as it passed from the Episcopal church to the cemetery, were hundreds of women and children who had lost fathers, brothers and husbands during the war. It moved up Braddock Street a few blocks to Piccadilly Street and then east to Market Street before finally turning east onto Boscawen Street before entering the cemetery. The gathering was, according to McVicar, a "long column of people (the longest ever seen of citizens of Winchester)." She continued: "The Unknown dead had been placed in the large mound, but there was no monument there then. Upon the mound, 14 mourning maids placed their wreaths and flowers." The mound contained 829 unknown Confederate dead from the Battles of Cool Spring, Second Kernstown, Third Winchester and Cedar Creek.

Since Union authorities had banned the use of the Confederate flag, a flag with one white and two red stripes was substituted. Instead of Confederate flags, flowers were placed on all 1,747 marked graves. On June 6 each year since, the townspeople have gathered at the site and held a memorial service. Small Confederate battle flags eventually replaced the flowers on the graves, but each year one of the original red-and-white flags is placed at the entrance to the cemetery.

Another unintended economic benefit of the war was the flurry of reunions that took place in Winchester by veterans of both sides. Monuments to the regiments and states that fought around the town were built and dedicated over the next forty years, and veterans gathered by the hundreds, and sometimes thousands, for these ceremonies. Local members of the General Turner Ashby Camp, United Confederate Veterans, in Winchester did everything they could to help provide accommodations and refreshments and make them feel welcome, whether they were Union or Confederate.

For the ones who bore the losses and cared for the wounded and dying, life began anew after Appomattox. Most prospered but some did not. For many of the most prominent families in Winchester, the war cost them everything. The Barton family was ruined financially by the war and forced to sell their beloved country home and farm, Springdale. Strother Barton, who never fully recovered from his wound at the Battle of Mine Run, died in 1868 of pneumonia. In all, the Barton family lost three sons, a daughter, a son-in-law, a brother and a father during the war.

However, the story of their three surviving sons is one of triumph. Mrs. Lee, after being thrown out of town by Sheridan, settled in Baltimore, Maryland. There she helped two of the Barton sons get a new start in life. Randolph and Bolling Barton eventually settled in Baltimore and found success. Randolph became a doctor and Bolling a lawyer. Mrs. Lee never returned to Winchester, but upon her death in 1907, she was buried in Winchester's Mount Hebron Cemetery next to her husband.

Robert Barton, after the war, also traveled to Baltimore and spent a few weeks with the family of his old friend, Bob McKim, who had been killed at the First Battle of Winchester. He returned to Winchester and became a very successful lawyer, writing several highly acclaimed law books from his home on Washington Street. All three brothers lived into the twentieth century and fathered large families.

Robert Y. Conrad, although elected mayor of Winchester in 1864, was never allowed to serve in that office due to his vocal support for the Confederacy. He did, however, continue in his law practice and, at least in the eyes of his neighbors, was Winchester's leading citizen. He died in 1875, but the story of the Conrad family's tremendous contribution to their hometown did not end with his death.

Conrad's son, Holmes Conrad, after serving in the Confederate cavalry during the war, returned to Winchester and began a law practice. He rose to become one of the most successful lawyers in the town's history. His career included trying cases in front of the United State Supreme Court and serving as assistant attorney general of the United States and as solicitor general. It was his friendship with a certain Pennsylvania millionaire, however, that brought about his greatest contribution to his hometown.

Judge John Handley, a bachelor from Scranton, Pennsylvania, developed a close friendship with Conrad after the war, and both took a deep interest in Winchester's economic development. When Handley died in 1895, he left a large portion of his wealth to Winchester with the express purpose of building a public library and a public school system. With so much money at stake, Holmes Conrad spent the majority of his remaining years fighting in court for Handley's bequest.

Before his death in 1915, Conrad was able to see one of the three crowning jewels of his work: Handley Library was opened in 1913. A decade later, after a massive building project, John Handley High School was opened, and a few years later, Douglas School for Winchester's African American community opened its doors. The library today serves not only Winchester but also Frederick and Clarke Counties. Douglas School operated until the

John Handley High School, Winchester, Virginia. *WFCHS.*

1960s, when it was converted into a community center after integration. Handley High School, after a recent renovation, is still serving the community and remains Winchester's most cherished institution.

Holmes Conrad's son, Robert Y. Conrad Jr., served as a major in the 116th Infantry Regiment in World War I and is buried in France after posthumously receiving the Distinguished Service Cross for valor at the Battle of Argonne Forest. Through three generations, Conrad family members placed service to their community, in both war and peace, as their primary function. Although Robert Y. Conrad Jr.'s grandfather refused to "illuminate" for General Winfield Scott Hancock, his descendants have illuminated the minds of countless children in Winchester and the surrounding area for nearly one hundred years.

Cornelia McDonald, after sacrificing so much for her children during the tumultuous days she spent in Winchester during the war, eventually settled in Kentucky with her sons. She died in 1909 and is buried next to her husband, Angus McDonald, at Hollywood Cemetery in Richmond, Virginia. After being interred in Mount Hebron upon her death in 1862, McDonald's baby, Bessie, was later moved to Hollywood Cemetery and rests beside Cornelia and Angus.

Reverend James Graham and his wife, Fanny, continued to live at the Kent Street Presbyterian manse well into the twentieth century. A look at one of the old city directories shows that the two even had a telephone late in life. Stonewall Jackson's widow, Mary Anna, made frequent visits to Winchester after the war, staying with her old friends the Grahams. The Kent Street and Loudoun Street churches eventually merged, but Graham, perhaps the most respected minister in the history of Winchester, still held services at the old church until his death.

Perhaps the most devastating results of the war were the number of widows and orphans created by the fighting, as well as the number of young women who never married because so many of the men their age were dead. Susan Jones, the widow of the much beloved Major Frank Jones, never remarried. Unable to care for their farm, Carysbrook, where she and Frank lived before the war, she moved in with her brother and helped him run a private school for boys. She also spent her time after the war teaching and raising not only her own children but also the orphans of Confederate soldiers. At one point, twenty children graced her home. Late in life, she moved back to Carysbrook and died there in 1905.

Among those who never married were Julia Chase, Gettie Miller, Tillie Russell and Mary Tucker Magill. Chase, although one of the most devoted Unionists in Winchester, still maintained the respect of her fellow townspeople for the rest of her days. Upon her death in 1906, some of the most distinguished citizens of Winchester acted as pallbearers. She was buried in Mount Hebron Cemetery just a few yards from the grave of Robert Y. Conrad.

Anne Tucker Magill, the fun-loving mother of Fanny Graham and Mary Tucker Magill, opened a school shortly after the war. She died in 1876 and was buried at Mount Hebron. Her daughter, Mary, was not only an educator but also became a celebrated author. In 1877, she published a history of Virginia that was used as a textbook in many of the schools across the state. She also authored several widely read novels and magazine articles. She died in 1889 and was buried next to her mother.

Tillie Russell never sought any publicity for her role at the Battle of Rutherford Farm. But when John Esten Cooke wrote an article about it and her name was revealed to the public, an artist named Minor Kellogg came to Winchester to meet her. After taking him to the battlefield and showing him the spot where she kept her all-night vigil with Randolph Ridgely, Kellogg painted a picture of her with the wounded soldier. That led to the sketch by Oregon Wilson, bringing her national fame.

She spent the rest of her life in service to the Confederate veterans she had cared for on a daily basis during the war and was a founder and active member of the Stonewall Memorial Association, which created the Stonewall Cemetery at Mount Hebron. When she died on February 18, 1897, the Winchester paper wrote of her: "No one in this city was held in higher esteem and no one was more universally beloved." The article continued by recounting in great detail the story of her famous "Night on the Battlefield." Although today she is still recognized as one of Winchester's greatest heroes, she is also representative of hundreds of Winchester women who like Tillie were angels every day in the hospitals and on the battlefields during the war.

Of all the women of Winchester during the Civil War, perhaps the most famous among local citizens was the indomitable Kate McVicar. A pioneer of female journalism, she wrote columns for the *Winchester Journal*, the *Winchester Times* and the *Winchester Evening Star* under the pen name of "Nemo." Her columns were diverse, some giving advice to young ladies on proper conduct and manners and others concerning issues of local and national interest.

Mrs. Harriet Griffith Ellis, taken later in life, Winchester. *WFCHS.*

Her most popular pieces, and the ones that have endured, were the ones she wrote about her experiences during the Civil War. She freely published letters, comments and other items concerning Winchester's part in the war and was generous in her praise of the men and women who had served honorably, regardless of which side they favored. Privately, she wrote poetry, and although very little of it was ever published, it is still read today by interested visitors to the Handley Library, where her poetry is kept. She died on February 20, 1920, and is buried in Mount Hebron Cemetery among the heroes about whom she wrote so eloquently.

Harriet Griffith Ellis traveled to Louisiana and then Texas with her husband, who continued to serve on General Sheridan's staff after the war. The couple eventually settled in Melrose, Massachusetts, where Harriet became involved in the temperance movement and the women's suffrage movement. She died on January 23, 1919. Her obituary in the *Melrose Free Press* noted that "her public life testifies to her sterling character, her strong, womanly worth, and her hearts desire to be of help to all good causes." It went on to add that "[i]n private life her many traits of sweetness and tenderness attracted to her many friends."

Captain William Ellis, a member of General Philip Sheridan's staff and the husband of Harriet Griffith, Winchester, Virginia. *WFCHS.*

One of Harriet's friends, Rebecca Wright, was not always remembered with the same universal love, at least in Winchester. To her Unionist friends, she was a hero who changed the course of the war, helped save the Union and freed the slaves. Many in Winchester, however, considered her a traitor. No one knew of her actions concerning the Third Battle of Winchester until Sheridan presented her with a watch. With that gift, she was forced to leave Winchester forever. With Sheridan's help, however, she obtained a job in the Treasury Department in Washington, where she worked for almost half a century. In 1871, she married William C. Bonsal. She died in 1914 and is buried in Washington, D.C.

Kate Sperry, with Aunt Sortia, made the harrowing journey through a dying Confederacy safely. In North Carolina she discovered that she truly loved her Dr. Hunt, and they were married in December 1864. Beginning the war as a lovely young girl who loved the attention given to her by a legion of admiring soldiers, she matured quickly in the troubled town. The daily care of the wounded, the loss of so many friends and the deeply depressing experience

Kate Sperry's grave in Ripley, Mississippi. *WFCHS.*

of watching her grandfather slowly die affected the words in her diary. During the last few months that she lived in Winchester, it changed from a witty and humorous record of daily life to a bitter tirade against all things Yankee.

Once in North Carolina, though, she returned to her old self. Moving to Mississippi with her husband, she died at the young age of forty-three in 1886 and is buried in Ripley, Mississippi. Shortly after the war, she and her husband traveled to Winchester to say a final goodbye to her many friends and relatives in town. Her last diary entry, written on December 1, 1865, revealed her growth: "We've been married one year tonight and I still think I have the best husband of any one and the dearest one in the world."

Through all of the years since the surrender at Appomattox, Winchester and the Shenandoah Valley have not forgotten their Civil War history, and one twentieth-century story demonstrates that. On June 6, 1944, the Second Ranger Battalion captured Pointe du Hoc, Normandy, in one of the most daring attacks in American history. President Ronald Reagan immortalized the battalion forty years later when he called them "[t]he boys of Pointe du Hoc, the men who took the cliffs."

Hackwood as it appears today, where Colonel John H.S. Funk was wounded during the Third Battle of Winchester. *THL.*

This picture of Hackwood was taken shortly after the Third Battle of Winchester, September 19, 1864. *U.S. Army Heritage and Education Center, Carlisle, Pennsylvania.*

The story, however, does not end there. What is usually left out of their story is that the rangers were nearly wiped out by a vicious counterattack by the Germans later that day and into the night. At dawn on June 7, nearly out of ammunition and suffering horrific casualties, the "boys of Pointe du Hoc" were in serious danger of being thrown off those cliffs into the Atlantic Ocean. Suddenly, a regiment of American soldiers appeared. They had broken through the German defenses on Omaha Beach.

They were not just any soldiers, though. They were members of the 116th Infantry Regiment, all of whom were from the Shenandoah Valley. Like their ancestors, nearly one hundred years before at Chancellorsville under Stonewall Jackson, the regiment launched a devastating flank attack and routed the Germans. Since its creation, the 116th Infantry Regiment, then and today, has sported a nickname. From the gentle, rolling hills around the Henry House near Manassas to the tangled central Virginia wilderness, to the blood-soaked fields around the Hackwood farm, to the Battle of Argonne Forest (where they were commanded by Robert Y. Conrad's grandson), to Omaha Beach (where the soldiers from Bedford County, Virginia, suffered more casualties than any county in the United States that day) and, finally, to the street fighting in Iraq today, they are, and always will be known as, the Stonewall Brigade.

Bibliography

Manuscripts

STEWART BELL JR. ARCHIVES, HANDLEY REGIONAL LIBRARY, WINCHESTER, VIRGINIA
Allan Tischler Collection, Winchester–Frederick County Historical Society (WFCHS).

Ben Ritter Collection, WFCHS.

Frank B. Jones Diary, Louisa Crawford Collection, WFCHS.

Graham Family Collection, WFCHS.

Harriett Griffith Diary, Harriett Griffith Collection, WFCHS.

John Peyton Clark Journal, Louisa Crawford Collection, WFCHS.

Julia Chase Wartime Diary, 1861–64, Julia Chase Collection, WFCHS.

Kate McVicar Collection, Handley Library (THL).

Kate Sperry's "Surrender? Never Surrender!" manuscript, edited by Lenoir Hunt, Rare Book Collection, WFCHS.

Margaretta Barton Colt Collection, THL.

Margaretta "Gettie" Miller Diary, Godfrey Miller Collection, WFCHS.

Mrs. Hugh Lee Diary, Mrs. Hugh Holmes Lee Collection, WFCHS.

Reverend Benjamin F. Brooke Journal, 1837–63, Benjamin F. Brooke Collection, WFCHS.

Richard Duncan Collection, WFCHS.

BOOKS OF PRIMARY MATERIAL

Jackson, Mary Anna. *Life and Letters of General Thomas J. Jackson (Stonewall Jackson)*. Harrisonburg, VA: Sprinkle Publications, 1995.

Macon, Emma Cassandra Riely, and Reuben Conway Macon. *Reminiscences of the Civil War*. Cedar Rapids, IA: privately published, 1911.

Magill, Mary Tucker. *Women; or Chronicles of the Late War*. Baltimore, MD: Turnbull Publications, 1871.

McDonald, Cornelia. *A Diary With Reminiscences of the War and Refugee Life in the Shenandoah Valley, 1860–1865*. Nashville, TN: Cullen and Ghertner, 1935.

Russell, William Greenway. *What I Know About Winchester: Recollections of William Greenway Russell, 1880–1891*. Edited by Garland Quarles and Lewis Barton. Winchester, VA: Winchester–Frederick County Historical Society, 1972.

ARTICLES

Graham, J.R. "Some Reminiscences of Stonewall Jackson." *Winchester–Frederick County Historical Society Journal* 11 (1998–99): 77–103.

Riggs, David F. "Robert Young Conrad and the Ordeal of Secession." *Virginia Magazine of History and Biography* 86 (July 1978): 259–74.

Winchester–Frederick County Historical Society Journal 8. "The Break-Up of a Nation: Robert Y. Conrad Letters at the Virginia Secession Convention" (1994–95): 1–95. Published by the Winchester–Frederick County Historical Society, with the permission of the Virginia Historical Society.

NEWSPAPERS

Melrose Free Press.
Winchester Evening Star.
Winchester Republican.
Winchester Virginia.

SECONDARY SOURCES

Colt, Margaretta Barton. *Defend the Valley: A Shenandoah Family in the Civil War.* New York: Oxford University Press, 1994.

Delauter, Roger U. *Winchester in the Civil War.* Lynchburg, VA: H.E. Howard, Inc., 1992.

Driver, Robert J., Jr. *The 1st and 2nd Rockbridge Artillery.* Lynchburg, VA: H.E. Howard, Inc., 1991.

———. *1st Virginia Cavalry.* Lynchburg, VA: H.E. Howard, Inc., 1991.

Duncan, Richard. *Beleaguered Winchester: A Virginia Community at War, 1861–1865.* Baton Rouge: Louisiana State University Press, 2007.

Foreman, Michael. *Some Worthy Women.* Winchester, VA: Winchester–Frederick County Historical Society, 2007.

Frye, Dennis E. *2nd Virginia Infantry.* Lynchburg, VA: H.E. Howard, Inc., 1984.

Gaines, William H., Jr. *Biographical Register of Members Virginia State Convention of 1861, First Session.* Virginia State Library, Richmond, Virginia, 1969.

Johnston, Wilbur S. *Weaving a Common Thread: A History of the Woolen Industry in the Top of the Shenandoah Valley.* Winchester, VA: Winchester–Frederick County Historical Society, 1990.

Joint Committee of Hopewell Friends, assisted by John W. Wayland. *Hopewell Friends History, 1734–1934, Frederick County, Virginia.* Strasburg, VA: Shenandoah Publishing House, Inc., 1936.

Quarles, Garland. *Occupied Winchester, 1861–1865.* Winchester, VA: Winchester–Frederick County Historical Society, 1991.

———. *Some Old Homes in Frederick County, Virginia.* Winchester, VA: Winchester–Frederick County Historical Society, 1999.

————. *Some Worthy Lives: Mini-Biographies*. Winchester, VA: Winchester–Frederick County Historical Society, 1988.

————. *Winchester, Virginia, Streets, Churches, Schools*. Winchester, VA: Winchester–Frederick County Historical Society, 1996.

Reidenbaugh, Lowell. *33rd Virginia Infantry*. Lynchburg, VA: H.E. Howard, Inc., 1987.

Riggs, David F. *13th Virginia Infantry*. Lynchburg, VA: H.E. Howard, Inc., 1988.

Robertson, James I. *Stonewall Jackson: The Man, the Soldier, the Legend*. New York: Macmillan Publishing, 1997.

Wallace, Lee A. *5th Virginia Infantry*. Lynchburg, VA: H.E. Howard, Inc., 1988.

Wert, Jeffrey D. *"A Brotherhood of Valor": Common Soldiers of the Stonewall Brigade, CSA, and the Iron Brigade, USA*. New York: Simon and Schuster, 1999.

————. *From Winchester to Cedar Creek: The Shenandoah Valley Campaign of 1864*. Carlisle, PA: South Mountain Press, Inc., 1987.

Index

About the Author

Jerry Holsworth is the assistant archivist for the Handley Regional Library in Winchester, which is under the auspices of the Winchester–Frederick County Historical Society. The Winchester–Frederick County Visitor Center also employs Jerry to give tours on the Civil War three to four times a year. Jerry is the author of several articles for *Blue and Gray Magazine* and *Civil War Times*, and he is a sportswriter for the *Winchester Star*, the *Loudoun Times-Mirror* and the *Northern Virginia Daily*. His work has also appeared in the *Washington Times*, *Cobblestone Magazine* and *Potomac Magazine*. Jerry was a park ranger at Antietam National Battlefield. From 1998 to 2000, Jerry was also the manager of George Washington's Office Museum in Winchester. He currently lives in Winchester.

Visit us at
www.historypress.net